PAST AND PRESENT

History, identity and politics in Ireland

Brian Walker

The Institute of Irish Studies
Queen's University Belfast

First published 2000
The Institute of Irish Studies
Queen's University Belfast
Belfast

© Brian Walker

British Cataloguing-in-Publication Data. A catalogue record for this
Book is available from the British Library.

ISBN 0 85389 769 7

Printed by W.G. Baird Ltd, Antrim
Cover design by Dunbar Design

CONTENTS

ACKNOWLEDGEMENTS   vii

INTRODUCTION   ix

CHAPTER 1   1
Remembering the siege of Derry:
the rise of a popular religious and
political tradition, 1689–1989

CHAPTER 2
The lessons of Irish history: 29
the continuing legacy of the 1798 rebellion
and the United Irishmen

CHAPTER 3
Public holidays, commemoration and identity   79
in Ireland, north and south, 1920–60

CHAPTER 4
The burden of the past: history and politics   101
in Northern Ireland

Notes   123

Index   143

ACKNOWLEDGEMENTS

During the writing of this book I have been helped by many people and organisations. I am much indebted to the staff of the library of Queen's University Belfast, the Linen Hall Library and the newspaper section of the Belfast Central Library. For their valuable comments and encouragement I am very grateful to Don Akenson, Allan Blackstock, Colm Croker, Marianne Elliott, David Fitzpatrick, David Hayton, Neil Fleming, Jane Leonard, Gillian McIntosh, Margaret Smith and Bill Vaughan.

I have delivered earlier drafts of the chapters in this book as conference papers or public lectures over the last few years. I am appreciative of the critical and helpful response which I received over them. Chapter one was given originally in 1997 as a paper at a conference in Derry on the siege of Derry, sponsored by the Community Relations Council. Material from chapter two formed the main part of one of my Ardilaun lectures at Alexandra College, Dublin, in 2000. Chapter three was given in 1997 at University College Cork at a conference on the Ireland of Eamon de Valera. The final chapter, updated here, was delivered in 1999 at a conference on Irish Studies at the University of Olomouc in the Czech Republic.

I am very grateful to my colleagues at the Institute of Irish Studies for their encouragement and support. I am especially indebted to Catherine Boone for her assistance in completing the text. Patricia Horton and Margaret McNulty helped greatly at the final copyediting and publishing stage. My last and deepest words of thanks must go to my wife Evelyn and our children Katherine and David who have supported me uncomplainingly throughout the writing of this book.

INTRODUCTION

At the end of his novel *Trinity*, the writer Leon Uris remarks that in Ireland there is no future, only the past happening over and over. It is often said that people in Ireland live in the past. It is a commonplace view among outside observers and residents alike that the present conflict in Northern Ireland has deep historical roots. President Bill Clinton has talked a number of times of 'ancient enmities' in Northern Ireland. On the eve of the referendum on the Belfast Agreement in May 1998, an editorial in the *Belfast Telegraph* talked of a new partnership between the peoples of these islands, British and Irish, 'that will replace 800 years of enmity with trust and friendship.' The editorial concluded: 'We have a chance to break free from the past and go for the future.'

The essays in this book challenge this view of the relevance of the past in Ireland. It is argued that history is actually no more important in Ireland than elsewhere. At the same time it is clear that many people here do refer to and use the past more than is common in most other societies. They employ the past to help explain the present and to justify their actions. People value certain historical traditions which seem important to their sense of identity. In Ireland, north and south, communities often possess a strong awareness of history. What must be realised, however, is that this popular historical sense is usually selective and can be influenced as much by people's current needs as any immutable link to the past.

The first two chapters in the book examine two historical events, the siege of Derry, 1688–9, and the 1798 rebellion, which are commemorated annually, and which impart important historical lessons for many today. At first sight the continuation of these commemorations would seem to strengthen the argument in favour of the importance of the past. Detailed study, however, shows that popular appreciation and understanding of these historical events has changed considerably over the years, in response to contemporary events and new political conditions. Focussing on four commemorative events, the third chapter explores how people's appreciation of their community identity and historical sense changed in both parts of Ireland, even in only the short period of four decades examined here.

The widespread belief in the importance of the past for the present in Ireland has considerable consequences. In the case of the situation in Northern Ireland, the critical role attributed to the importance of the past, which often involves a selective use of history and myths, has helped perpetuate the conflict. Chapter four includes a study of how people both within and from outside Northern Ireland constantly use this historical framework to interpret the nature of the problem. An attempt is made to explain why this happens and what its consequences are. It is argued here that an exaggerated and selective use of history has had a detrimental effect on efforts to find a peaceful resolution to the very real contemporary problems faced in Northern Ireland. The idea that the conflict is based on age old hatreds and long term historical roots is not only incorrect but damaging. In its challenge to the importance of perceived notions of history, this book asserts the primacy of people to control the making of their own history today.

1

REMEMBERING THE SIEGE OF DERRY:
THE RISE OF A POPULAR RELIGIOUS AND
POLITICAL TRADITION, 1689–1989

Commemoration of the siege of Derry, 1688–9, is an important annual concern for many protestant and unionist people today in Northern Ireland. Well attended parades, church services and other ceremonies are held in Derry on two special dates every year. On or near 18 December the closing of the city gates at the beginning of the siege is remembered while on or near 12 August the relief of the city at the end of the siege is recalled. These acts of commemoration are attended not just by citizens of Derry but by people from many parts of Northern Ireland. Supporters come from County Donegal as well as from Canada and Great Britain. In recent years there has been controversy and conflict over the parades in Derry and also over the parades of supporters in Belfast and Dunloy, County Antrim, on their way to Derry. This chapter will explore these commemorative events and will seek to explain why and when they have come to play such an important part in the annual religious and political calendar of Northern Ireland. Special attention will be paid to the role of the clubs of the Apprentice Boys of Derry in the demonstrations. The period covered runs from the end of the siege until the tercentenary celebrations of the event in 1989.

Many commentators have remarked on the significance of the siege of Derry and its commemoration for the protestant and unionist community. It has been claimed that 'ever since' 1689 there has been significant celebration of the event in a manner similar to that experienced today.[1] Jonathan Bardon, in his history of Ulster, has written: 'For the protestants of Ulster this epic defence gave inspiration for more than three centuries to come'.[2] Referring to various dates in the protestant historical calendar, such as the rebellion of 1641 and the Battle of the Boyne of 1690, the social anthropologist Anthony Buckley has commented: 'Of all these historical events, the siege has the greatest symbolic significance'.[3] Journalist David McKittrick, in his book *Despatches from Belfast* has remarked about the siege: 'In three centuries it has never lost its potency and immediacy as a symbol for unionists, for they believe that the enemy is forever at the gate, waiting for the sentry to fall asleep'.[4] In his analysis of the roots of the conflict in Ulster, *The narrow ground*, A.T.Q. Stewart sees the siege as central to the historical consciousness and experience of protestants from the seventeenth century to the present.[5]

From these comments and the evidence of the ongoing annual parades in Derry, it is clear that the siege and its commemoration play a vital part in contemporary Northern Ireland. Questions remain, however, about these popular celebrations. Has the siege always been remembered in the way that it is today, and have these celebrations always enjoyed such wide support? What do we know about the origins of traditions associated with the commemoration of the siege, such as the burning of an effigy of the 'traitor', Lundy? The clubs of the Apprentice Boys of Derry are responsible now for running the annual events, but it will be valuable to know how long they have performed this role. How has support grown for the Apprentice Boys since their formation? Why do the celebrations remain important today for large numbers of the population of Northern Ireland? This chapter will seek to answer these questions. The subject of the reaction from catholic and nationalist quarters to the commemorations will not be investigated here: this matter is dealt with in a number of recent articles by Tom Fraser.[6]

The role of the siege in protestant culture from the late seventeenth to the twentieth century has been the subject of a number of modern studies. Sam Burnside, for example, has looked at how the siege has been celebrated in drama, verse and prose.[7] Ian McBride has examined early efforts to commemorate the siege and has analysed tensions within the protestant community over this matter.[8] He has shown how divisions existed between presbyterians and members of the Church of Ireland until the 1880s when he believes that a broad protestant consensus emerged and the annual commemorations in Derry drew on support across Ulster, thanks to the efforts of the Apprentice Boys of Derry clubs. This chapter will concentrate on growth of support for the commemorations from the 1880s, although attention will also focus on the earlier period in order to highlight the great changes that took place. McBride's book spends little time on developments after the 1880s, and there is no detailed study of the growth of these commemorations in the last one hundred years, apart from some useful studies on a number of the Apprentice Boys of Derry clubs, written by the Derry local historian C.D. Milligan in the decade 1945–55.[9]

I

For most of the first one hundred years after the siege, it seems that public commemoration of the events of 1688–9 was sporadic and without wide support. The earliest, reliable, evidence of celebration of the siege in the eighteenth century is an entry in the diary of Dr William Nicolson, bishop of Derry, 1718–27, written on 1 August 1718, the anniversary (under the old calendar) of the ending of the siege: 'I read prayers (first and second services) at Londonderry: Col. Michelburne's bloody flag being hoisted the first time, on the steeple. Evening, splendid treat in the tholsel, fireworks and illuminations'.[10] Over the next half century there are few references to the event: sources are limited owing to the absence of a Derry newspaper until the 1770s. There is no evidence of popular commemoration of the siege apart from the holding of occasional services or dinners in honour of the event.[11] This lack of support for commemoration of the siege is probably due in part to bitter

presbyterian/Anglican conflict which emerged locally in the immediate aftermath of the siege and which was heightened by early
eighteenth-century legislation against presbyterians, such as the Test
Act of 1704 which banned them from the corporation until
1780.[12] By the last decades of the eighteenth century such intra-
protestant rivalry had eased but not ceased.

Reports in the local press in the 1770s confirm that there had
been some earlier celebrations of the siege, but also that these had
lapsed and were only renewed towards the end of the eighteenth
century. In August 1772 the *Londonderry Journal* carried a resolution from a local guild which declared gratitude to the city's mayor
because he had 'revived' the 'ancient custom of commemorating the
equally glorious and memorable deliverance of this city...'[13] The
newspaper describes the scene in Derry on 1 August, when the bells
were rung, the crimson flag or banner (denoting the 'maiden city')
was displayed on the cathedral steeple and the mayor, corporation
and freemen processed to a service at the cathedral, followed later
by a dinner and other festivities. The mayor declined to assemble
the citizens for the August commemoration in 1773; thereafter this
event was marked annually. Until 1775 the anniversary of the shut-
ting of the gates was a matter of 'private conviviality' but from this
date it became a public event: in December 1788 an effigy of the
traitor of the siege, Colonel Robert Lundy, was burned for the first
time.[14] By the 1770s there is also evidence of the involvement of
clubs or societies of local citizens, which can be seen as forerunners
of the nineteenth-century Apprentice Boys' clubs, although in the
late eighteenth century these groups usually met privately to celebrate the siege, were often short–lived and played a minor role in
the celebrations, organised normally by the corporation. From the
mid 1770s units of local volunteer corps and the city garrison
joined the commemorations.

In 1788 and 1789 there were special centenary anniversary commemorations.[15] In early December 1788 the closing of the gates
was remembered by church services in both the cathedral and a
presbyterian church, followed by a civic procession, a military
parade and the burning of Lundy's effigy. The celebrations also

involved a special dinner, attended by catholic clergy as well as town dignitaries. In August 1789 commemoration of the breaking of the boom on the river Foyle by the *Mountjoy* and the consequent relief of the city included a sizeable procession to the cathedral which included not only the members of the corporation but the catholic bishop and his clergy, as well as the presbyterian clergy and elders. On both these occasions the siege was commemorated as a great blow against tyranny which brought liberty to people of all Christian denominations. At the service in the cathedral the preacher, Rev. George Vaughan Sampson, urged that the message from the example of their forefathers was not just 'Glory be to God in the highest' but also 'on earth, peace, goodwill towards men'.[16] In late eighteenth-century Ireland, with the rise of a tolerant Irish patriotism, the events of 1688–9 were seen as part of the Glorious Revolution with its constitutional benefits for all, and embraced presbyterians, members of the Church of Ireland, and catholics.[17]

II

The next half-century,1789–1839, witnessed important changes in how the siege was commemorated in Derry. The closing of the gates in December became a more popular event to be celebrated than the ending of the siege in August. Military units from the city garrison played a part in the celebrations until the 1820s, when their participation ended, owing to government policy not to be involved in events which were seen as partisan: locally raised units of volunteers, such as yeomanry, continued to parade on these occasions until the 1830s.[18] A monument, consisting of a column and statue, in honour of the siege governor, Rev. George Walker, was erected in 1828. There is some evidence of catholic involvement in the celebrations in the early years of the nineteenth century but this had stopped by the 1830s.[19] Reflecting the rise of protestant/catholic tension in Ireland in the early nineteenth century, the siege came to be seen increasingly as a protestant symbol.[20] Some protestants, such as the editor of the *Londonderry Standard* (founded in 1832), continued to view the siege as a victory of liberty for all, but by the

1830s the commemorations were dominated by those who regarded the siege solely as a protestant victory.

By the 1830s the civic authorities were no longer involved (except
on special occasions) in the annual commemorations which were
now run by clubs of Apprentice Boys. The first nineteenth-century
club of the Apprentice Boys of Derry (so named after the apprentice boys who shut the city gates in the face of the forces of James
II in 1688) was formed in 1813. The club, however, was based , in
Dublin and drew its support from well-off supporters of the union
who had an interest in Derry: it survived until the early twentieth
century, but met privately in Dublin and had little or no influence
in Derry.[21] In 1824 the No Surrender Club of Apprentice Boys was
formed in Derry. The Ordnance Survey memoirs of the early 1830s
recorded the existence of three such clubs in the city, but noted that
they were losing influence and would 'doubtless become gradually
extinct.'[22] In 1835 a new club, with the broad title of the
Apprentice Boys of Derry Club, was founded in Derry. The first
rule of the club declared the aim of celebrating the anniversary of
the siege while the second stated that in the formation of the club,
members were not 'actuated by factions or sectarian feeling, which
we consider would be at variance with the cause of civil and religious liberty, the celebration of its establishment being the special
purpose for which our society was instituted'.[23]

Celebrations of the 150th anniversary of the siege were markedly
low-key, compared with the centenary. In December 1838 the closing of the gates was marked only by the flying of flags, a salvo of
guns, the burning of Lundy and a 'bottle and glass party' in the corporation hall, presided over by the sheriff. It was noted that no
catholics were present and most of the protestants were of the
'humbler class'.[24] 'Bottle and glass parties' were a common feature
of celebrations in this period and involved participants bringing
their own alcohol: they were replaced by more respectable tea parties and soirées in the 1840s.[25] None of the Derry papers gave
much coverage to the August celebrations in 1839, which involved
a short march by some Apprentice Boys together with supporters from Enniskillen, and which seems to have been poorly

supported.[26] The Belfast press carried no reports at all of the occasion.

The following fifty years saw significant growth in the popularity of these commemorations and in the fortunes of the Apprentice Boys. A number of new clubs were formed, and these proved to be longer lasting and better organised than their predecessors. While the No Surrender Club and the Apprentice Boys of Derry Club were the only Derry-based clubs to survive from the pre-1839 period, some new clubs were formed in honour of heroes of the siege: the Walker Club (1844), the Murray Club (1847), the Mitchelburne Club (1845, revived 1854) and the Browning Club (1854, revived 1861).[27] The growth of the clubs in the 1840s and 1850s probably reflects local demographic developments resulting in a rise in the number of catholic inhabitants, which meant that by the 1850s protestants were no longer a majority in the city.[28] Around 1859 a general committee was established to co-ordinate the clubs and the celebrations. The post of 'governor', as head of the committee and the clubs, was created in 1867, although it lapsed in 1871 and was then restored in 1876. The clubs were Derry-based, and before the late 1880s it seems that most members were born or lived in Derry.[29] Club rules, as in the case of the Apprentice Boys of Derry Club, did not exclude outsiders, but since membership required all members to attend club meetings once a month this made it difficult for people outside Derry to retain membership.[30]

By the late 1850s commemorations in Derry were well attended, a situation which reflected more than just a rise in local interest. As Aiken McClelland has pointed out, crucial to the rise in popularity of these events was the arrival of the railway in Derry.[31] The opening of the Derry/Coleraine line in 1852 and the Derry/Strabane line in 1854 meant that many more people could now attend the demonstrations. The Party Processions Act which banned political parades, and was operative between 1850 and 1871, did not prevent these commemorations because they were seen as civic rather than political events and the marchers avoided using political banners and party tunes, although there was conflict on a number of occasions in this period between Apprentice Boys and the

authorities as well as Derry catholic residents over some of the ceremonies connected with the anniversary of the siege. The press in
the late 1850s and 1860s recorded the attendance at the celebrations of considerable numbers of visitors, both onlookers and participants.[32] William Johnston, elected to parliament in 1868 as an
independent protestant conservative candidate for Belfast, attended
regularly from 1860.[33] By the 1870s the August celebrations had
become more popular than those in December. While membership
of clubs was restricted mainly to Derry residents, a category of honorary membership had grown up, in spite of opposition from at
least one club.[34]

An important stage in the development of the organisation of
Apprentice Boys' clubs was the opening of a purpose-built hall in
Derry in 1877 for the use of all the clubs. The idea of such a centre was first floated in the late 1860s, the foundation stone was laid
in 1873, and five years later a hall, in memory of the original
Apprentice Boys of the siege, was opened. Costing £3,250, the new
Apprentice Boys' Memorial Hall provided a meeting place for all
the clubs, a room for initiation services into the institution and an
assembly hall for speeches after the 12 August church service. A
contemporary newspaper account described the new hall as 'in the
style prevalent in the fortified and baronial residences of Scotland
and this northern province in the sixteenth and seventeenth centuries, chosen as being most suitable to its memorial character, and
the events with which it is associated'.[35]

In 1877 the general committee of the associated clubs adopted a
common form of initiation service for all new club members.[36] The
order of precedence of the clubs in the annual parades was decided
by the 1880s, after considerable debate. A march of clubs around
the walls and the firing of cannon, along with the cathedral service,
were regular features of the 12 August commemorations by this
time. In 1888–9 the bicentenary of the siege was marked by extensive celebrations which involved not only the Apprentice Boys but
also the city corporation. The usual commemoration ceremonies
were well attended and other features of the event in August included a mock breaking of the boom on the river by the *Mountjoy*, a

replaying of the original event two hundred years earlier. These activities involved both Apprentice Boys' clubs and many visitors.[37]

While most of the customs and practices associated with the siege commemorations, which are evident in the twentieth century, were in place by this stage of the late nineteenth century, it must be stressed that the extent of popular involvement was still limited. Evidence given in 1869 to an enquiry about riots in Derry revealed that total membership of all six Apprentice Boys' clubs in that year stood at only around three hundred ordinary members and two hundred honorary members, while a letter of 1867 from J.C. Ferguson, governor of the Apprentice Boys' clubs, appealing for funds for the new hall, referred to '300 active members'.[38] A newspaper account in the *Northern Whig*, 13 August 1870, described the August parade as totalling about one thousand, including two hundred Apprentice Boys and four bands. Numbers of Apprentice Boys had probably grown by the bicentenary but since full membership was still confined largely to Derry residents it is unlikely that the total of Apprentice Boys had increased significantly. Sizable numbers of people from the surrounding countryside and further afield did come to view or even to join the parade, but they were not involved formally. Attempts had been made in the 1870s to establish clubs outside the city, but these proposals met with rejection from the general committee of the Apprentice Boys: 'no charter will be granted for use outside the city of Londonderry'.[39] By 1889, however, the important decision had been taken to allow the establishment of external local clubs, although at the bicentenary celebrations it seems that only a small number of such clubs was in existence.[40]

As regards the composition of the Apprentice Boys' clubs in this period, we may note a comment of the *Londonderry Sentinel* editorial that the August 1889 bicentenary celebration was 'emphatically a people's commemoration' with few 'prominent leaders'.[41] William Johnston M.P. was one of the few leading politicians involved regularly in these annual events in Derry.[42] The government enquiry of the late 1860s had revealed that the Apprentice Boys' clubs were made up mainly of 'respectable tradesmen', were generally supportive of the conservative party in Derry and included both presbyterians and members of the Church of Ireland.[43] Efforts in the 1860s, however, to alternate the August anniversary service between the Church of Ireland cathedral and a presbyterian church foundered when First Derry presbyterian church refused to allow the clubs to bring their banners into the church: after this the cathedral was the main site for these services.[44] Many middle class Derry presbyterians supported the liberal party in the late 1860s and although this party collapsed in Derry in the early 1870s, there is little evidence of their active involvement in the commemorations.

Liberalism remained strong among rural presbyterians in County Londonderry and elsewhere in Ulster until the 1885–6 general elections, when most former liberals and conservatives joined a new unionist movement.[45] Nonetheless, even in the late 1880s there is no sign of new, mass presbyterian involvement in the siege celebrations or the Apprentice Boys clubs. The main presbyterian liberal paper in Ulster, the *Northern Whig*, gave the August 1889 bicentenary events a mere six inches of column space, in contrast to the extensive coverage in the *Belfast News-Letter*, evidence, perhaps, of residual bad feeling between presbyterians and members of the Church of Ireland over the history of the siege.[46]

Commemoration of the siege in places outside Derry and by organisations other than Apprentice Boys' clubs are relevant here. A survey of the contemporary press does reveal some celebration of the event in a range of places in Ulster in the period between the fiftieth anniversary and the bicentenary in 1889. We read of instances such as an Orange dinner in Belfast on 18 December 1855 to mark the relief [sic] of the city, an Orange demonstration near Lurgan on 12 August 1873 to celebrate the siege and the burning of an effigy of Lundy in Larne on 18 December 1886.[47] Sometimes 12 August was used as the occasion for special Orange events such as the opening of an Orange hall, as in Portadown in 1875.[48] During these years, however, the celebrations were not commonplace; they were neither widely supported nor organised annually. The major exception was in County Fermanagh where on

12 August, from the 1840s, the siege of Derry was commemorated frequently along with the battle of Newtownbutler (its anniversary was also 12 August) and other Fermanagh events of the 1688–9 wars.[49]

At the bicentenary of the siege on 12 August 1889 there were major Orange celebrations only in Fintona, County Tyrone, and Kesh, County Fermanagh.[50] The attendance at Kesh was described as large, with a special train bringing 'brethren' from counties Tyrone and Donegal as well as County Fermanagh, but numbers were much lower than in Derry. One of the speakers at Kesh declared that: 'They were descendants of the men who stood upon Derry's walls and who fought at the battles of Newtownbutler and Lisnaskea, and who manned the banks of the Erne. The descendants of these men would never let themselves be trampled upon'.[51]

Clearly then, the period 1839–89 witnessed an important increase in the popularity of the siege celebrations and in the role and membership of the Apprentice Boys' clubs. Demographic shifts in Derry probably aided this development, while the improvement of transport facilities was a significant economic element which helped to open up the event to supporters from a much geographic area than before. The fact that Orange marches were banned during the 1850s and 1860s, while siege commemoration parades were allowed in Derry, may help to explain the rise in popularity of the latter. The continued growth in support for the celebrations in the 1870s and 1880s undoubtedly reflected the growing political tensions and the emergence of unionist/nationalist confrontation throughout Ireland in this period. This helped to give a new relevance to the story of the siege, especially for Derry protestants.

Until the late 1880s, however, these annual commemorations appealed only to a limited number of people, as is reflected in the scarcity of siege celebrations outside Derry (even in 1889), the relatively low number of outside participants at the Derry events, and, particularly, the limited membership of the Apprentice Boys' clubs, drawn largely from the protestant inhabitants of Derry and its neighbourhood. The decision of the general committee of the Apprentice Boys in the late 1880s to allow the setting up of local branches of the clubs was a momentous one. It meant that whereas the Derry siege had become an important symbol for many protestant residents of Derry (to be celebrated annually in a special way), it could now take on a similar significance one for others elsewhere. Why the decision to allow this was taken at this particular point is not clear. Probably, because of the emergence of strong national parties and the major issue of home rule, Derry unionists now saw themselves as members of the larger unionist and protestant community. This decision would have major consequences for the level of broader involvement in the siege celebrations.

III

The period 1889–1939 witnessed a complete transformation in the amount of popular support for the commemorations in Derry and the Apprentice Boys' clubs. The key to this change was the decision taken to allow the Derry-based clubs (now known as parent clubs) to establish branch clubs outside the city. All members continued to be initiated within Derry's walls. No annual returns are available for the total membership of the Apprentice Boys' clubs, but a good idea of the growth of the movement can be gained from newspaper accounts of the number of clubs and the figures of annual initiation. It is usually possible to obtain from newspapers accurate information on the names and numbers of the clubs. Annual figures for total numbers initiated are difficult to find in the early period 1889–1923, because members of the various clubs were initiated at different times of the year, but from 1923 there were usually combined initiations for all club members at the August commemorations, and so reliable figures of numbers initiated are often, although not always, available in the press after 1923. Rarely in this period does the press record figures for the number on parade or the total number present.

Initially, and perhaps surprisingly, the growth of these branch clubs was slow. At the August 1889 celebrations, three branch clubs, all from Belfast, joined the parade.[52] By August 1900 there were just eight branch clubs (four from Belfast, two from County

Antrim, one from County Armagh and one from County Down)
present at the August commemorations, although this meant that
there were now more branch than parent clubs (seven in 1900).[53]
Celebrations in August 1914 (for the 225th anniversary of the
siege) saw a particularly low turnout because of transport restrictions arising from the outbreak of war in Europe.[54] Two years earlier, however, the August parade included seventeen branch clubs,
of which there were six from Belfast, three from County Antrim,
one from County Armagh, five from County Down and two from
County Londonderry.[55] Clubs received a charter when no less than
thirteen members had been admitted to full membership of the
Apprentice Boys; initiation had to occur within Derry's walls.
During this period the December celebrations were confined to
parent clubs.[56] Records for the period 1900–14 show that a small
number of branch clubs was established in Canada and Scotland.[57]
From 1911 the general committee of Apprentice Boys' Clubs was
allowed to nominate six members to the Ulster Unionist Council.[58]
During the first world war the annual commemorations continued,
although in a restricted form.

In 1920, riots in Derry led to all parades being banned, but the
usual church services were attended by members of the Apprentice
Boys' clubs.[59] In 1923 a press report on the August parade recorded the presence of seventeen branch clubs, a figure similar to club
numbers present in 1912: upwards of three hundred new members
were initiated in August 1923.[60] From this time on, however,
expansion in the number of clubs and initiations occurred rapidly.
In 1924, for the first time, a presbyterian minister preached in the
cathedral at the August anniversary. The next day, the *Northern
Whig*, unusually, devoted an editorial column to the celebrations,
declaring that 'every loyalist in the province loves and claims a patriotic interest in the stones of Derry': this new degree of interest by
the *Northern Whig* may be explained by the fear expressed in its editorial that under the threatened redrawing of the border Derry
would be lost to the Free State.[61]

Following the erection of a war memorial in the Diamond in the
1920s, the laying of wreaths by the leading party in the parade

became an important feature of the commemorations. From the
early 1920s new members were initiated at a joint ceremony usually held during the August commemorations. In 1927 the Baker
Club was revived, so that there were now seven parent clubs.
Branch club numbers on parade at the August commemorations
increased to thirty one in 1924, fifty one in 1930, and eighty in
1936. In 1924 several hundred new members were initiated, but by
1936 annual initiations totalled eight hundred.[62] By 1939 the
number of branch clubs totalled ninety three and in that year seven
hundred new members were initiated.[63]

Analysis of distribution of branches on parade over this period
reveals how the Apprentice Boys' organisation had spread throughout Northern Ireland. In August 1923 the 17 branch clubs came
from the following areas: Belfast 6, County Antrim 2, County
Armagh 2, County Down 2, County Londonderry 3 and County
Tyrone 2.[64] The 51 branch clubs on parade in August 1930
belonged to: Belfast 7, County Antrim 7, County Armagh 7,
County Down 9, County Londonderry 8, County Tyrone 11 and
County Donegal 2.[65] By the two hundred and fiftieth anniversary
parade in August 1939 the 93 branch Clubs were to be found in:
Belfast 7, County Antrim 16, County Armagh 10, County Down
18, County Fermanagh 2, County Londonderry 13, County
Tyrone 15, County Donegal 6, Scotland 4 and England 2.[66] The
sudden growth in Donegal branches in the 1930s is probably
explained by the restrictions on Orange parades in Donegal after
1932. The Scottish branches came from Govan, Patrick,
Springburn and Glasgow, and the English branches from Liverpool
and Birkenhead. These figures relate to the number of branches on
parade and so may underestimate slightly the total number of clubs
in existence, as some, especially those from Canada and Scotland,
did not always attend.[67]

Although the number of clubs in Belfast during the period
1921–39 increased only by one after the founding of a Belfast
branch of the newly revived Baker Club, their membership grew
rapidly. In 1925 a charter was granted to create a Belfast and
District Amalgamated Committee to co-ordinate the Belfast

branches.[68] In 1939 the Belfast branch of the Browning Club had three hundred members on parade in Derry, the largest turn out of any club or branch.[69] Plans were drawn up in this period to build a hall for the Belfast clubs, but this never materialised and the clubs continued to avail of Orange halls, as did the other branch clubs.[70] A Mid-Ulster Amalgamated Committee was in existence by the early 1930s. By the mid 1930s the Apprentice Boys' organisation was holding parades on Easter Monday in different centres around Northern Ireland for parent and branch clubs.[71]

In 1936 the foundation stone for a large extension to the Apprentice Boys' Memorial Hall in Derry was laid by the city's lord mayor, Captain J.M. Wilton.[72] Costing £30,000, the new premises were opened in 1938 by Viscountess Craigavon to provide extensive additional accommodation which included a large assembly hall to seat nearly two thousand people, rooms for the meetings of clubs and local Orange and Black lodges, and new social facilities. In this period we can note the initiation of some prominent politicians into the Apprentice Boys' clubs, although apart from Derry politicians, they seem to have played little regular part in the commemorations. In 1933, for example, Sir Dawson Bates, minister of home affairs in the Northern Ireland government, and W.H. Price, attorney general of Toronto, Canada, were initiated into the Murray Club.[73]

Celebrations in Derry city in 1938–9 to mark the 250th anniversary of the siege were very extensive, probably reflecting concern over Northern Ireland's constitutional position, a fact apparent from the 1938 general election which was fought on the issue. The December 1938 commemoration of the closing of the gates was better attended than usual, with a special train bringing supporters from Belfast.[74] The main focus for the 250th anniversary was at the 12 August 1939 demonstrations for the anniversary of the relief of the city. The *Londonderry Sentinel* reported that 'all morning until noon, Apprentice Boys and their friends, who grow more numerous every year, poured into the city from every part of Northern Ireland and the border districts of Eire'.[75] A total of twenty one ordinary and special trains, about one hundred buses and many cars brought upwards of twenty thousand people to the city.

The huge procession in 1939 consisted of one hundred Apprentice Boys' clubs (both parent and branch clubs) and around one hundred bands. At the service in the cathedral, the preacher was Dr James Little, a presbyterian minister and one of two union-ist MPs for Down constituency. His sermon was primarily a reli-gious one but he referred to current threats from the southern government and militant republicans:

> To all who are seeking in one way or another to undermine our state we send today this message from the historic walls of Derry, that nei-ther to politician nor terrorist will we ever consent to surrender any portion of the inheritance which God has entrusted to us.[76]

In its editorial the *Londonderry Sentinel* stressed the relevance of the siege in face of contemporary threats at home and abroad.[77]

An important feature of the period 1889–1939 was the growth in celebration of the event in centres outside Derry on 12 August by organisations other than the Apprentice Boys. Whereas in August 1889 the only important demonstrations took place at Kesh in County Fermanagh and at Fintona in County Tyrone, both organ-ised by the Orange Order, by the early 1900s there were additional demonstrations in both counties, and supporters from counties Donegal, Cavan, Londonderry, Armagh and Monaghan were involved, sometimes on their own and sometimes in joint demon-strations.[78] By 1910, however, organisation of these 12 August anniversary celebrations was almost entirely run by preceptories of the Royal Black Institution, rather than the Orange Order, although Orange lodges sometimes attended the parades. On 12 August 1910 there were demonstrations not only at a number of centres in Tyrone and Fermanagh, but also at Annaghmore, County Armagh and in Cavan town.[79]

During the 1920s and 1930s well attended demonstrations were held by the Royal Black Institution on 12 August in different loca-tions in south and mid Ulster.[80] In the years after 1932 such parades ceased in Counties Cavan, Monaghan and Donegal owing to local republican opposition, but 'brethren' from these counties attended parades in Northern Ireland.[81] At the 250th anniversary of the siege on 12 August there were demonstrations run by the Black Institution in Cookstown, Drumquin and Ballygawley, in County Tyrone, and Irvinestown, in County Fermanagh. Those attending came from all the nine Ulster counties, except Down and Antrim.[82]

The increase in support for the Apprentice Boys' organisation and its celebrations in Derry, as well as parades elsewhere, clearly reflects the growing significance of the Derry story in the new political and religious confrontations of post-1886 Ireland. The fact that the rise of such support was strongest after 1921 may be related to the new, exposed situation of Derry on the border of Northern Ireland. It may also be the result of a general rise in interest in this period in loyal orders, such as the Junior Orange Association, founded in the 1925.[83] It has been argued that support for the Orange Order declined in the period 1921–39, but it is possible that this was because individuals were joining other organisations, such as the Apprentice Boys.[84] While membership of the Apprentice Boys' organisation was undoubtedly influenced by the political situation, the religious situation was also significant. By the 1920s the commemorations in Derry no longer included meetings for political speeches, but centred largely on the religious services held in the cathedral. Increased support for the Derry parades may be seen as evidence of a growth in popular protestantism, uniting different denominations, as well as a rise in political unionist activity. Interesting comment on the new pervasiveness of the Derry story can be found in the account of celebrations and anniversaries in County Fermanagh in the history of Enniskillen, written by W.C. Trimble and published in 1921.[85] He claimed that Orangemen in Enniskillen on 12 July and 12 August 'while they celebrate the deeds of other places, ignore the resolve of their own townsmen to close their East Bridge to King James' soldiers in December 1688 and to their own great victory at Newtownbutler...' He hoped that his history would help to cure 'this ignoring of the Enniskillen men by Enniskillen men'.

IV

During the second world war the public celebrations of the siege in Derry were cancelled by the Apprentice Boys' general committee. In August 1946, at the first peacetime demonstration since the war, a record number of 2,500 to 'nearly 3,000' members were initiated at ceremonies which, according to the *Londonderry Sentinel*, 'continued from 9.00 am till 5.00 p.m'.[86] The Sentinel also noted that 'over 10,000 free drinks were served by the Londonderry Temperance Council from thirteen specially erected stalls along the processional route'. In the same year it was reported that the procession contained seven thousand Apprentice Boys and ninety bands.[87] In 1947 the preacher at the August cathedral service, Rev. J.G. MacManaway, M.P. for Derry city at the Northern Ireland parliament and Church of Ireland clergyman, declared:

> We in Ulster have our own Holy Place, our own religious shrine to which our history as Protestants forever joins us. The Protestant shrine of Protestant Ulster is forever Derry. We do not meet together to provoke anybody or criticise any man's faith. But, just as our forefathers before us, we are resolved that we shall not be driven out of this country by political pressure or economic measures to deprive us of our freedom and our faith.[88]

During the late 1940s and 1950s the numbers of members initiated frequently reached or passed one thousand.[89] Press reports on the commemorations after the war no longer list the names of all the clubs taking part and only occasionally do they record their numbers. We may note, however, that in 1950 and 1958 it was reported that one hundred and twenty clubs were present at the August parades, along with a similar number of bands.[90] Actual numbers of Apprentice Boys in the parade varied between five and eight.[91] Given the large number of annual initiations it seems clear that all members did not attend every year. It is difficult to give precise figures of all those present but press estimates ranged between thirty and forty thousand.[92] Attendances could be affected by whether or not demonstrations were held on a Saturday.

The number of parent clubs increased to eight with the revival of the Campsie Club in 1950. This period also saw the formation of a number of amalgamated committees for different areas: Scotland (1946), Ballymena and district (1948), South Down, later County Down, (1948), Coleraine and district (1948), South Derry and East Tyrone (1954). In 1963 an amalgamated committee for south-west Ulster was formed to cover Monaghan, Cavan, South Donegal, Fermanagh and West Tyrone.[93] The general committee of Apprentice Boys was extended to include representatives from these committees. Until the 1950s the December parades were attended primarily by members of parent clubs with only a few representatives from other clubs but after this dare more members from outside attended the commemoration of the closing of the gates, although numbers were still much lower than in August.

In 1961, centenary celebrations for the founding of the Browning Club were the occasion for the first methodist minister to preach in the cathedral.[94] During the 1960s the number of annual August initiations seems to have dropped to around five hundred, but at this time December initiations became more popular than before. The parades continued to attract large numbers of Apprentice Boys, bands and onlookers. On 15 August 1962, the *Londonderry Sentinel* reported that:

> The parade was so long that it filled the entire two and a half-mile-long processional route from the Diamond, via Carlisle Road, the Bridge, Duke Street... The last contingents had not left the Diamond when the head of the procession had returned and was passing through the Diamond to the walls.

In Scotland Apprentice Boys' clubs celebrated only with church services until 1959 when the first open-air rally was held at Caldercruix. Since then the Scottish amalgamated committee has organised its main rally on the third Saturday in May.[95]

By the 275th anniversary of the siege in 1964, the number visiting the city on 12 August was put at thirty five thousand, a figure which was slightly down from the total of forty thousand two years earlier, when the August commemoration fell on a Saturday.[96] The number of those initiated was recorded as around five hundred in August 1962 and August 1964 (one hundred others were initiated in December 1964).[97] In August 1964 it was reported that the two and a half mile long parade contained more than one hundred clubs, five thousand Apprentice Boys and one hundred bands, and took one hour and ten minutes to pass Carlisle Square.[98] It was estimated that on the same occasion nineteen Ulster Transport Authority trains, one hundred and sixty Ulster Transport Authority buses and three thousand cars were required to bring the visitors to the city. The Lough Swilly Company brought five hundred visitors from County Donegal. The press reported that there were representatives from Canada, Scotland, Liverpool and Philadelphia, as well as contingents from Counties Donegal and Monaghan.

By the 1960s the initiation of prominent politicians was commonplace although few of them seem to have played a regular part in commemorations. Two prime ministers of Northern Ireland, Lord Brookeborough and Captain Terence O'Neill, were initiated in 1960 and 1964 respectively. Brian Faulkner, minister of commerce, was initiated in 1966: that same year, writing in the Ulster Unionist Council year book, he welcomed the involvement of young people in politics, stating that 'going right back to the Apprentice Boys our young men and now young women too have been quick to sense the need for action and to give a lead'.[99]

Although it is difficult to give a complete picture of the strength of the Apprentice Boys' movement in this period, because newspapers no longer record the names of branches, we are able to gain an important insight into the organisation's composition from an official Apprentice Boys' printed list of branch clubs, branch club secretaries and local places of meeting for the year 1971.[100] The list records a grand total of one hundred and seventy eight clubs, but notes that in nine cases the clubs made no return of information, which implies that they were defunct. As regards these one hundred and seventy eight clubs, their distribution was as follows: Belfast 16, County Antrim 31, County Armagh 16, County Down 28, County Fermanagh 5, County Londonderry 22, County Tyrone

35, County Donegal 7, Scotland 14, England 2, Canada 2 and USA 1. In comparison with the figures for 1939, this record reveals a number of interesting developments, especially the increase in the number of Scottish and Belfast clubs. This 1971 list records eight amalgamated committees as well as a general committee of twelve officers and thirty three members. Clearly this picture shows considerable growth. To some extent, however, as in the case of Belfast, it may simply reflect the breakaway of clubs from existing clubs into new clubs rather than a real increase in the numbers of Apprentice Boys actually involved.

Since 1970 the form of the siege commemorations has changed considerably. After riots in the city in 1969 following the 12 August parade, a ban was imposed on Apprentice Boys' parades during 1970 and 1971, although services continued in the cathedral. From 1972 to 1974 the August procession was restricted to the Waterside. In 1975 the parade was allowed into the walled city during the August commemoration, but it was confined to the upper part of the city and marches around the walls continued to be banned: only from 1995 have parent clubs been allowed to march around the city walls again (in 1997 the march took place later in the year). The burning of Lundy's effigy from Walker's monument was banned by government order in 1970, and the monument itself was blown up in 1973, but this did not end the December siege celebrations. Since 1970 the effigy of Lundy has been burned in nearby Bishop Street. The December parades were also banned during 1970–5, but have continued in a restricted form since then. In the mid 1970s the formal link between the Apprentice Boys general committee and the Ulster Unionist Council was broken when the nomination of six members to the Council was ended. In 1984 a demonstration of Apprentice Boys was held in London to protest against the change of the name of the city council from Londonderry to Derry. During these decades several new amalgamated committees were formed, including one for England.

It is not easy to assess numbers of clubs, Apprentice Boys on parade, or new members initiated, during the two decades 1969–89, because press reports are scanty in their information on these subjects; figures for initiations are also more difficult to find because during this period the ceremony was performed at various times, not just in December and August. As regards numbers of those initiated, it seems that 1960s levels have been maintained, if we judge by figures for August 1979 (400) and August 1985 (600): in 1982 640 were initiated in August and 100 in December.[101] Figures for those present at the commemorations in August ranged from five thousand in 1972 to twenty thousand in 1985: the security situation undoubtedly effected these numbers.[102] Two of the few press references to the number of Apprentice Boys in the procession put them at seven thousand in 1977 and ten thousand in 1988, while several Apprentice Boys' sources put full membership at eleven to twelve thousand by 1988.[103] The numbers of bands participating increased during the period from one hundred and thirty nine in 1977 to one hundred and sixty in 1989.[104]

There are no accounts in the press of the number of clubs on parade during these decades, but we do know that there were one hundred and seventy eight in existence in 1971 and, according to the official Apprentice Boys' tercentenary brochure, over two hundred by 1988.[105] Although this latter figure has been questioned there is evidence of the growth of new clubs in these years. In August 1982, for example, there were new clubs at the parade from Newmills (County Tyrone), Ballinakillen (County Donegal), Clough (County Down), Portrush (County Antrim) and Dalry (Scotland).[106] A special feature of this last period has been the increase in the number of clubs in Scotland and England.

The tercentenary of the siege in 1989 was the occasion of extensive celebrations in the city. The Apprentice Boys' organisation co-operated with the nationalist city council in various functions and commemorative events. In August characters in period costume re-enacted scenes from the siege, and a mock breaking of the boom by the *Mountjoy* was staged.[107] Local councils elsewhere, such as Omagh and Lisburn, organised civic receptions for representatives of the Apprentice Boys' organisation. In May a parade of Apprentice Boys was held in Edinburgh to mark the tercentenary. At the cathedral service in Derry on 12 August 1989 the preacher,

Rev. James Kane, spoke of the many deaths and destruction of the previous twenty years.[108] In an official Apprentice Boys' tercentenary brochure, which referred to both the general political situation and the local reduction of the number of protestants on the west bank of the city, the chairman of the tercentenary committee wrote: 'the siege of Derry is, in many senses, still going on'.[109] Other publications at this time included a book on the siege by Peter Robinson, M.P., in which he declared: 'For three centuries Londonderry has been the symbol of Protestant resolve and dogged determination to stand against any threat to its inhabitants and their way of life.'[110]

Continued expansion of the Apprentice Boys' organisation in the period 1939–89 can be explained by a number of factors. Clearly the siege of Derry remained a potent symbol for more and more unionists and protestants in Northern Ireland. For the first two decades of this period, however, a special factor was the shift in emphasis by the Royal Black Institution in its August parades from 12 August to its other day of parades on the last Saturday of August. During the 1950s in all counties except in Fermanagh demonstrations on 12 August ceased outside Derry, thus freeing members of the Black Institution and Orange supporters to join the Apprentice Boys clubs and to attend the Derry celebrations. Sometimes Black preceptories would mark 12 August with church services but this date was no longer the occasion for major Black parades. Continuation of the 12 August celebrations in County Fermanagh may be explained by a rise in local interest in the battle of Newtownbutler (also celebrated on 12 August) and other county Fermanagh events of 1688–9.

Expansion in the number of clubs and members since 1969 should be seen as part of the growing interest in loyal orders and parades in the unionist community as a result of the 'troubles' in Northern Ireland. Dr Neil Jarman has stated: 'In recent years, and perhaps particularly since the signing of the Anglo-Irish Agreement in 1985, protestants have felt their constitutional position, and therefore their sense of national identity, more threatened than at any time since partition'. As Jarman goes on to point out, one

response to this crisis of identity 'has been to parade more frequently in local areas, and also to organise more parades for more
events'.[111] The rise in outside support for this particular event is
perhaps attributable to the symbolic loss of Derry to nationalist
control and the reduction in the number of protestants in Derry. In
the face of this shift, there is a need felt to show protestant and
unionist solidarity.

V

The siege of Derry is recalled today by large numbers of the protestant and unionist community in Northern Ireland who annually
celebrate the event in well attended parades, church services and
other ceremonies in Derry. Although it is believed by many, including the writers at the beginning of this chapter, that there has always
been such deep interest in the subject, the evidence of the annual
commemorations over the years would suggest otherwise. It is not
true that 'ever since' 1689 the event has been celebrated in a fashion similar to that today: commemorations in Derry have evolved
considerably over the last three hundred years. We do not know
how far memories of the siege remained in the consciousness of
protestants, but evidence of their concern, as expressed in their
degree of support for these commemorations in Derry and elsewhere, does not suggest that the siege has been either a major source
of inspiration or of great symbolic value 'ever since' 1688–9. From
our knowledge of celebrations of the siege in Derry, it is clear that
there was a substantial period when there was little popular commemoration of these historic events, that there were times when the
siege was seen in an inclusive light, and, of course, that also there
were long periods when the siege served as a great protestant and
unionist symbol, although the number of people involved in this
last stage greatly altered over time. The most marked growth in
popular support for commemoration of the siege was not in the
early nineteenth century, nor indeed in the late nineteenth century,
but in the period after 1921. The extent of the change which

occurred in the popular appreciation of the siege can be seen in the sharp contrast between celebrations in August in Derry in 1839 and a century later in 1939. On the former occasion small numbers of locals, with some visitors from Enniskillen, were involved. By the latter date the *Londonderry Sentinel* could report: 'For this year's celebration they came from almost every town and district in Northern Ireland to join with their brethren in the maiden city.'[112]

The shape, degree of support for and meaning of the siege of Derry have undergone many changes over three centuries. Most of the elements of celebration and ritual associated with the commemorations today originate in the late eighteenth and nineteenth centuries. Many aspects of the modern siege celebration can be located to certain dates of origin. By the time of the bicentenary the commemorations in Derry had taken on most of the characteristics with which we associate these events today. However, the numbers involved in these annual celebrations were still very limited. The formation of the Apprentice Boys of Derry was essential for the growth in popular support for these events. The majority of Apprentice Boys' parent clubs today date from only the 1840s or 1850s. Under their control, and owing both to local factors and national issues, the siege celebrations grew in popularity. From a very low degree of support in the 1830s and 1840s the Derry commemorations had become well attended by the 1880s. At this stage, however, formal involvement in these annual parades was limited largely to protestant residents of Derry.

An important change in the organisation's rules in the 1880s allowed the creation of local clubs of Apprentice Boys, outside the city. While some growth in club numbers ensued in the following two decades, real expansion occurred only after 1921. From a figure of 9 parent and local clubs in 1889, numbers grew to 23 in 1923, 100 in 1939, 178 in 1971 and over 200 in 1989. It is only in the last seventy-five years that it can be said that the siege of Derry commemorations enjoyed significant involvement from the wider Protestant and unionist community in Northern Ireland. For members of that community, in their present-day situation, the story of Derry has served as a meaningful lesson in their political and religious lives. This signals a significant shift from earlier centuries when the siege served as a strong protestant symbol for a limited number of people, and an even greater change from when it had served as an inclusive symbol for protestants and catholics.

As current commemoration of the siege of Derry makes clear, the siege of Derry is a key element in the contemporary protestant and unionist sense of tradition or history. It is important to realise, however, that what is regarded as 'traditional' does not come to us unaltered through time, transmitted naturally, from the date of origin of the tradition or the event on which it is based. Organisations, people and events influence and alter the traditions we use. In this case the formation and growth of the Apprentice Boys of Derry, the influence of churchmen and politicians, and events such as the setting up of Northern Ireland in 1921, all had a direct bearing on how the siege of Derry has been commemorated. Contemporary affairs influence significantly how popular a particular tradition is.

The siege of Derry has developed into an important tradition because, especially in this century, it has been viewed by more and more people as a deeply relevant symbol and source of inspiration, particularly in light of the political and religious conflicts in their society. Each generation has interpreted the siege to suit their current needs. To see tradition in such a way is not to devalue it. Instead it shows that often what others may regard as antiquarian or a relic from the past is rooted in present reality. Such understanding emphasises the importance of traditional commemorations. At the same time it also warns against the belief that these traditions are unchanging and fixed in time, a stance which can result in a failure to adjust effectively to modern circumstances and new events.

There has been considerable debate among historians about how traditions are formed and the ways in which they develop. Some historians have emphasised the roots of these traditions while others have stressed the modern situation which affects the way the traditions are taken up and become widely accepted. Eric Hobsbawm has talked of the 'invention of tradition' and has interpreted the rise of traditions as a response in the late nineteenth century to modern developments in communication, industrialisation and the political enfranchisement of the mass of the people.[113] In the Irish context, the importance of the origin of tradition, as opposed to the importance of the new conditions, has been emphasised in differing degrees by various historians. The present study shows how various aspects of the siege of Derry tradition fell into place during the eighteenth and nineteenth centuries, which accords with those who place emphasis on the strength of long-standing traditions. At the same time, however, the small number involved in this tradition over most of the early period has been stressed. Numbers involved were more substantial by the late nineteenth century, but it was only the political and religious conditions of post-1921 Northern Ireland that caused the larger protestant and unionist community to be actively involved. Therefore modern conditions were vital for the spread and survival of this tradition. Even the emergence of the home rule crisis in 1885–6 and again in 1912 was not enough to generate really wide interest in the Derry story. Besides the general social, political and economic changes, as emphasised by Hobsbawm, it was the particular circumstances of post-1921 Northern Ireland that caused greater participation in Derry commemorations, a popular involvement which has continued to this day.

For many members of the unionist and protestant community in Northern Ireland at present the siege of Derry is an important part of their sense of history. The traditions associated with their annual commemoration of the siege are regarded by them as an essential element in their cultural and historical identity. For those who march in Derry every year, as well as their supporters and friends elsewhere, this parade reminds them of a particular key episode in the history of their community. The significance of this event comes not from the length of its historical roots back to the seventeenth century but from conditions in the twentieth century which caused more and more people to see certain lessons of the siege as valid for their time. Much more important for the rise in popular interest and involvement in this event than any deep underlying historical consciousness has been the contemporary relevance of the

siege story in the modern day religious and political situation in
Northern Ireland, and the development and promotion of the
Derry commemorations by various individuals and organisations,
in particular the clubs of the Apprentice Boys of Derry.

2

THE LESSONS OF IRISH HISTORY :
THE CONTINUING LEGACY OF THE 1798
REBELLION AND THE UNITED IRISHMEN

References to the lessons or relevance of Irish history often occur in political discourse in Ireland, north and south. Present events are sometimes seen as the outcome or fulfilment of remote episodes in Irish history. The 1798 rebellion and the United Irishmen are good examples of historical subjects which later generations have recalled for instruction or inspiration. In the bicentenary year of 1998 commentators frequently declared a strong connection between the present and 1798. Many claimed that there was an important link between the current peace process and the ideals and example of the United Irishmen. After an ecumenical service in early September 1998 at the world's largest 1798 monument in Sydney, Australia, when news had come through of the Real I.R.A's ceasefire following the Omagh bomb, President Mary McAleese said: 'It seemed a particularly appropriate place to have that news, calling to memory the men of 1798 whose aspirations for Ireland, I think, hope and pray, are about to be realised in this generation and the next'.[1] At many of the ceremonies and church services to commemorate the 1798 bicentenary, reference was made to the United Irishmen's desire to unite protestant and catholic in a common purpose and identity.[2] Throughout Northern Ireland during 1998 members of unionist and nationalist communities shared efforts to commemorate 1798 and the United Irishmen.[3]

There have been, however, and still are, other interpretations of
the relevance of the 1798 rebellion and the United Irishmen. For
instance, the centenary of the rebellion in 1898 was celebrated as an
almost exclusively nationalist and catholic event. The example of
the United Irishmen influenced the republican leaders of the 1916
rising. Shortly before his execution, Sir Roger Casement stated: 'I
am not afraid to die, to join Wolfe Tone and Robert Emmet, and
hope that my death may one day help to make our country free'.[4]
In 1971 loyalist paramilitaries were responsible for blowing up
Wolfe Tone's statue in Dublin and destroying Jemmy Hope's gravestone in the graveyard at Mallusk in County Antrim. A republican
memorial at Kesh, County Fermanagh, erected in November 1998
to mark the bicentenary of the 1798 rebellion, lists three United
Irishmen and three I.R.A. men: of the latter, the first was killed in
the I.R.A. campaign of the 1950s and the other two during the
recent 'troubles'.[5] The inscription makes no distinction between the
eighteenth and the twentieth centuries.

Clearly then the relevance of the 1798 rebellion and the United
Irishmen can be interpreted in different ways. This chapter is concerned with examining the varying interpretations of these events
and looking at the context in which they emerge. We will explore
how the 1798 rebellion and the United Irishmen were recalled in
the two centuries after 1798. Attention will be paid to how they
were commemorated at the popular level and among political
activists. Their influence on subsequent political behaviour will be
considered as will writings on the subject. Particular attention will
be paid to Wolfe Tone who has become the best known figure from
this period and whose writings and sayings have been much quoted. How and when exactly did he gain this prominence? His declaration of August 1796 has been described as the most quoted passage of Irish history.[6] It described his aims:

> To subvert the tyranny of our execrable government, to break the con-
> nection with England, the never-failing source of all our political evils,
> and to assert the independence of my country – these were my objects.
> To unite the whole people of Ireland, to abolish the memory of all past
> dissensions, and to substitute the common name of Irishman in place

of the denominations of protestant, catholic and dissenter – these were my means.[7]

I

The first half century after 1798 saw little in the way of public com-memoration of the rebellion or of the United Irishmen. In the south loyalists in County Wexford celebrated the anniversary of the battle of Vinegar Hill with the burning of a 'liberty tree' on the hill, while at New Ross, County Wexford, they held parades to com-memorate the suppression of the rebellion. Events such as these, however, appear to have stopped by the 1820s.[8] On the rebel side in the south there seems to have been little such public commemo-ration. For the first two decades after 1798 the government remained alert to the possibility of a resurgence of popular support for the United Irishmen, but found nothing to give it serious con-cern. Although intelligence reports to Dublin Castle recorded vari-ous incidents, such as the turn out of large numbers at the funeral of Tone's father in 1805, there was no evidence of widespread revo-lutionary conspiracy.[9] After 1806 there was considerable agrarian unrest, especially in parts of Munster and Connacht, but the con-cerns of those involved were primarily economic. The appearance of a new secret society, the Ribbonmen, after 1811, did herald the appearance of a more politically alert movement of agrarian protest, but while this movement was linked to the protest aspect of the United Irishmen and their allies, the Defenders, it lacked coherent political ideas and effective leadership.[10] At the popular level of folk songs and oral tradition, memories of 1798 survived. John Devoy, a leading figure in the Irish Republican Brotherhood, described in the 1920s the ballads about the 1798 rebellion which had been common in his childhood in County Kildare in the 1840s.[11] Some well-known songs about 1798, however, such as 'Boolavogue', were written, not at the time of the rebellion, but afterwards in the late nineteenth century.[12]

Whatever their memories, the bulk of the former rebels and their descendents in the southern counties were willing to support the

constitutional politician, Daniel O'Connell, in his campaigns, first
for catholic emancipation and then for repeal. O'Connell had no
sympathy for the leaders or the ideals of the 1798 rebellion. His
attitude was coloured by a strong dislike of violence, based on his
experiences in revolutionary Ireland and France. In his diary in
January 1799 he recorded: 'Oh Liberty, what horrors are committed in thy name! May every virtuous revolutionist remember the
horrors of Wexford.'[13] In 1841 in a speech in Dublin he again crit-
icized those who had been involved in the uprising in 1798:

> As to '98, we leave the weak and wicked men who considered force and
> sanguinary violence as part of their resources for ameliorating our insti-
> tutions, and the equally wicked and villainously designing wretches
> who fomented the rebellion and made it explode [Camden's govern-
> ment]....We leave both these classes of miscreants to the contempt and
> indignation of mankind.[14]

For evidence of the wide support which O'Connell enjoyed we may
note Thomas Davis's rueful comment in the 1840s that the people
of Wexford 'sons of the men of "98"' were almost all repealers.[15] In
an account of his meeting in 1847 with Anne Devlin, who had suffered great privations because of her connections with Robert
Emmet and the United Irishmen, Luke Cullen recorded her deep
admiration for O'Connell.[16] Some of the leading United Irishmen
exiles in America also strongly supported O'Connell.[17]

In the northern counties there seem to have been little in the way
of public commemorations of the 1798 rebellion. The memorial in
Comber parish church to three members of the York Fencible
Infantry killed at the Battle of Saintfield, erected by fellow officers,
is a rare contemporary monument to 1798.[18] During the early
1800s there were reports to Dublin Castle of County Antrim meetings at which toasts were drunk to the memory of prominent
United Irishmen such as William Orr and Henry Munro and also
of continued interest in France among former rebel supporters in
Belfast. Otherwise, there was no evidence of political conspiracy or
unrest to seriously alarm the government.[19] Accounts of surviving
Defenderism in parts of Ulster in the same years also failed to

present any real concern to the authorities.[20] The emergence of Ribbonism in south and east Ulster post 1811 was not regarded as a serious political threat.[21] Descriptions of attitudes among former United Irishmen and presbyterians in County Antrim, as related in some of the ordnance survey memoirs of the 1830s, show that by this time many people had largely forgotten or ignored the events of 1798, although they retained an interest in social and political reform. For the parish of Templepatrick it was noted that: 'Since the lesson they got in 1798 they have meddled but little with party politics. They were then among the most disaffected in the kingdom....They are very independent in all their notions, but particularly on the subject of religion.'[22]

For both Henry Cooke and Henry Montgomery, prominent presbyterian ministers and leading public figures in early nineteenth-century Ulster, the 1798 rebellion left lasting and very different memories. In Cooke's case, the violence and anarchy of his childhood experiences of the United Irishmen in the Maghera area left in strong impressions which influenced his later conservative thinking.[23] In a speech in the 1830s he linked 1641, 1798 and the present.[24] The liberal Montgomery, whose his family home was burnt down by the military, took a positive view of the United Irishmen, which he expressed in an article in 1847: 'I am not ashamed to acknowledge that some of my kith and kin fought in the ranks of their country and I am proud to say that during the last forty years I have found my best, my clearest headed and warmest hearted friends among the United Irishmen of 1798.' At the same time he asserted that the principles of the United Irishmen, 'sound in themselves' had been 'applied and perverted' by 'wicked men' involving 'thousands in criminal projects under false notions of patriotism'.[25] Others, such as Mary Ann McCracken, retained a positive view of the United Irishmen, but took a different political attitude, due to new circumstances. In a letter written in the late 1830s she talked of:

> looking forty years back, and in thinking, too, of those who were gone, and how delighted they would have been at the political changes that

have taken place — which could not possibly, in their day, have been
anticipated by peaceable means — and of the improved prospects of
their country, now that the English in general, and particularly the
present ministry, have such feelings towards Ireland and Irish people.
...[26]

Writing later of his time in Ulster in the 1840s, Charles Gavan
Duffy remarked that 'the presbyterians ... knew no more of Tone
and Russell than of the Gracchi'.[27] In his own case, however, Duffy
recalled reading United Irish songbooks while he was growing up in
County Monaghan and he acknowledged the influence of the
United Irishman, C.H. Teeling, on him.[28]

Between 1798 and 1848 a number of books appeared on the subject of the United Irishmen's rebellion. These works reflect a wide
range of views on what actually happened and were sometimes
showed authors using 1798 on order to draw lessons for the
future.[29] On the loyalist side one of the first histories on 1798 was
Sir Richard Musgrave's two-volume account, published in 1801.
This book set events of the rebellion in the long term context of earlier risings against the crown going back as far as the twelfth century and in the more immediate setting of ongoing catholic hostility
towards protestants during the previous two hundred years.
Musgrave emphasised atrocities against protestants during 1798
and he denounced catholic clerical leadership of the rebels. In the
preface to the third edition(1802) of the history, Musgrave stated
his opposition to catholic emancipation because of what had happened in 1798 and in previous rebellions.[30] A different loyalist perspective was adopted by W.H. Maxwell in his 1845 history of
1798.[31] He blamed the outbreak of rebellion of 1798 on the influence of American and French revolutionary events and ideas, attributed the violence of that year to mob rule and rejected the idea of
a catholic clerical conspiracy. Maxwell believed that while 'all the
advantages promised from the Irish union may not yet have been
fully developed,' still the connection had proved useful, and so he
rejected repeal.

On the opposing side, published accounts also revealed a wide
range of views on 1798 and on its lessons. Early works, such as the

writings of James Clinch, at the behest of the catholic bishop of Ferns, James Caulfield, concentrated on refuting allegations of catholic clerical connivance in events; or, as in the case of the United Irishman, Edward Hay's publication, on blaming oppression and the failure to grant reform as the main reasons for the outbreak of the rebellion.[32] In these writings efforts were made to absolve the leaders of the United Irishmen of blame and to downplay revolutionary ideas; in some cases the authors may have feared arrest for sedition or involvement in the events of 1798. Published work from America, however, by some exiled United Irishmen, did place greater emphasis on political ideas in an unapologetic fashion.[33] The best example of this approach was the two-volume life of Wolfe Tone, based on memoirs and letters written before his death in 1798, and published in Washington D.C. in 1826.[34] Edited by his son, this account placed the rebellion in a full political and revolutionary context which set down Tone's beliefs in republicanism and the use of physical force. His son imposed his own censorship on these documents by removing references which were unfavourable to the catholic church and to the United States of America or which concerned his father's romantic adventures.[35] In the early 1840s R.R. Madden published an extensive seven-volume work on the United Irishmen and events of 1798.[36] Madden's volumes were very sympathetic to the United Irishmen but emphasized that the grievances which had caused rebellion in 1798 had now been dealt with: 'we have outlived the wrongs that made rebels of these men. In our times their descendants are possessed of rights, for the enjoyment of which they have reason to be good and loyal subjects. It is not only their duty, but their interest to be so.'[37]

Specifically northern accounts of 1798 are not plentiful in the half-century following the rebellion, although some general histories, such as the work of Musgrave and Madden, contained northern material. Shortly after the rebellion, from the safety of America, Saintfield United Irishman Rev. T.L. Birch and Belfast United Irishman Samuel Neilson published brief accounts of their experiences of 1798.[38] In an 1812 narrative of these events and his

imprisonment during them, the presbyterian minister Rev. Steele
Dickson described the parliamentary reform and catholic emancipation objectives of the early United Irishmen, blamed the insurrection on government excesses and denied that the rebellion was a
catholic conspiracy.[39] Historians today acknowledge Dickson as a
leading member of the United Irishmen movement, but in his
memoirs Dickson was very unclear about his role after 1796, probably because no formal charges of membership had been proved
against him and he was in financial need of the government fund-
ed *regium donum* for presbyterian ministers.[40] In 1825 the *Belfast
Magazine* carried favourable recollections of the Battle of
Ballynahinch by two eye witnesses, James Thompson and Rev.
Samuel Edgar, although both used pseudonyms, as did Mary Ann
McCracken in an article in the *Ulster Monthly Magazine*, 1830, on
Thomas Russell.[41] Another personal narrative of the 1798 rebellion
by a catholic United Irishman from Lisburn, Charles Hamilton
Teeling, was published in 1828.[42] He was unapologetic about his
role. Teeling also emphasised the early aims of reform and catholic
emancipation which had inspired the United Irishmen and claimed
that they had only turned to revolution because of the government's
response to their appeals. He stressed the union of protestant and
catholic in the United Irishmen and ignored claims of sectarian violence committed by them. In 1840 the autobiography of one of the
early leaders of the United Irishmen, Archibald Hamilton Rowan,
was published six years after his death. Rowan celebrated the early
idealism of the United Irishmen but described how he became dis-
illusioned with revolutionary politics after witnessing the violent
excesses in France to where he had fled at the height of the Terror
in 1794.[43]

Material on the rebellion was no more profuse on the side of
those opposed to the United Irishmen. In an 1803 volume published in Downpatrick, J.M. Johnston of Ballynahinch described
how 'the rebels came from the eastern part of the county, as the
plague of locusts came in Egypt....They afterwards came to
Ballynahinch, but few of the inhabitants joined them, but
fled....'[44] In George Benn's history of Belfast, published in 1823,

events of the 1790s in Belfast are described only briefly.[45] The influence of French revolutionary ideas is emphasised in Benn's as is the support of the townspeople for the crown and existing constitution. In 1838, on the fortieth anniversary of the rebellion, an article, which was generally supportive of the authorities, on the Battle of Ballynahinch, appeared in the *Down Recorder*, but otherwise this anniversary and the 50th anniversary went unmarked.[46] In the 1840s, however, two Belfast printed histories of the rebellion appeared. S.L. Corrigan's account of 1798, drawing largely on Musgrave's work, was published in 1844. The introduction to Corrigan's volume contained a warning that Daniel O'Connell and his followers were just as hostile to English and protestant interests in Ireland as the rebels had been in 1798 and readers were urged to join the Orange Order.[47] Samuel McSkimin's history, entitled *Annals of Ulster, or Ireland 50 years ago*, was published in 1849, several years after the author's death. Combining the use of a wide range of secondary sources and extensive local knowledge, McSkimin's account gave considerable details of northern events. A former member of the yeomanry he, nonetheless, showed a certain sympathy for the aims and members of the United Irish movement.[48]

The formation of the Young Ireland movement in the 1840s created new interest in the United Irishmen and the 1798 rebellion. On 1 April 1843 the Young Ireland newspaper *The Nation* carried a poem entitled 'The memory of the dead', eulogising the United Irishmen. Better known by its first line 'Who fears to speak of Ninety-Eight?', the poem was written by John Kells Ingram, because of his concern about the disregard for the United Irishmen shown by the O'Connellite movement.[49] The paper subsequently carried pieces on some of the United Irishmen and reprinted popular ballads first published in the 1790s in support of the United Irishmen.[50] At the same time we should not exaggerate the influence of 1798 on the writings of the Young Irelanders. The *Nation* carried articles on a wide range of Irish historical subjects.[51] A projected volume on Tone for their Library of Ireland series never materialised: other subjects covered included the patriot parliament

of James II and the Irish volunteers of 1782.[52] Young Irelanders
often urged the union of Irishmen of all creeds but rarely were the
United Irishmen cited as an example of this. In 1843 Thomas Davis
did write about the unifying example of the United Irishmen but
other articles in the *Nation* referred to the unity of Irishmen in
1782.[53] Among the collected poems of Thomas Davis, edited by
John Mitchel and published in 1868, there are a few pieces which
mention 1798, such as 'Tone's grave', but more common are poems
such as 'Song of the volunteers of 1782' and 'Lament for the death
of Owen Roe O'Neill.'[54] Before the 1840s few outside Tone's family had shown any interest in his grave at Bodenstown in County
Kildare. Davis visited the grave in 1843, after which he wrote his
poem on the subject. In the following year a number of Young
Irelanders erected a memorial slab at his grave.[55]

Until 1848 Young Irelanders aspired to a relatively limited independence for Ireland and did not advocate physical force.[56] During
1848, however, a number of Young Irelanders organised a rising. In
this they were greatly influenced by the revolutionary situation in
Europe, especially in France.[57] While the European example was
more important directly than that of 1798, the speeches and writings of the Young Irelanders at this period carry a number of references to the United Irishmen and the 1798 rebellion, which now
took on a new relevance. John Mitchel started a new paper, the
United Irishman. The first issue carried a quote from Wolfe Tone:
'Our independence must be had at all hazards. If the men of property will not support us, they must fall: we can support ourselves by
the aid of that numerous and respectable class of the community,
the men of no property.'[58] In April and May 1848 Mitchel used the
paper to addressed a series of letters to the protestants of Ulster,
'with the arms of freemen in all your homes and the relics of the gal-
lant republicans of ninety-eight for ever before your eyes.' He urged
them to rebel in arms against the government and fight for an independent republic, but to no avail.[59] At the same time James Fintan
Lalor announced that he wanted 'not the constitution that Wolfe
Tone died to abolish, but the constitution that Tone died to obtain
– independence; full and absolute independence for this island, and

for every man within this island'.[60] Not all those involved in support of the rising, which was a complete military failure, were doctrinaire republicans.[61] Afterwards, one of the leaders, William
Smith O'Brien declared:

> As for personal loyalty to the sovereign, I am not aware that I have ever
> during the course of my life uttered a word disrespectful to the queen
> and though in the event of a national war between Great Britain and
> Ireland I should have acquiesced in the establishment of a republic as
> the only form of government which circumstances have permitted. Yet
> my political principles have never been republican and I should have
> much preferred to any novel experiment a restoration of the ancient
> constitution of Ireland: the Queen, Lords and Commons of Ireland.[62]

In spite of the 1848 rising and the admiration of some of those
involved for the United Irishmen, during this first half century after
1798 events of that year were seen as of little relevance to most people in Ireland. There was little or no public commemoration of the
rebellion and while it was not forgotten, as the literature on the subject reveals, most of the population seem to have preferred not to
celebrate it or take inspiration from it, perhaps in part due to their
memory of the many thousands of deaths. Obviously, those northern presbyterian families who had been involved with United
Irishmen now clearly rejected their main political objectives, in the
main because of the new political and economic situation in Ulster,
and so had no interest in commemorating these events. Less obviously, those protestants whose families had been on the loyalist side
did not commemorate the year, as they did other years such as
1690, even though the outcome could be seen as a victory or 'deliverance' for them. The reason for this probably lies in the fact that
the rebellion had crossed denominational lines. Many United
Irishmen had been protestant and many military on the government side had been catholic. Among the catholic population there
was also little popular commemoration of 1798. Constitutional nationalism was the dominant political force in Ireland
during this half-century and most of its supporters preferred not to
commemorate the rebellion. Additionally, as for many loyalists, the

message of 1798 was not a clear-cut one, because many catholics, including Daniel O'Connell, had served in crown forces during the rebellion. Even for Young Irelanders, 1798 had only a limited appeal, perhaps due to an awareness that it had ended in the bloodshed and sectarianism.

II

In the late 1850s a secret revolutionary body, the Irish Republican Brotherhood, (I.R.B.), or the Fenian organisation, was founded in Dublin and New York. A number of its founders had been involved in the 1848 rising as Young Irelanders. Its single aim was independence for Ireland and it sought to achieve this by physical force.[63] With members in both America and Ireland it attempted a rising in Ireland in 1867, but with no success. The imprisonment of some of its leaders and the hanging of three members known as the Manchester Martyrs for the murder of a policeman, brought considerable public support for the Fenian movement for a time, but during this period of the 1870s and 1880s the vast bulk of Irish nationalists remained committed to the constitutional home rule party. In spite of these setbacks and lack of wide support the Fenian movement survived to maintain the ideas of political separation and physical force. How far exactly the movement in its early decades was influenced by the example of the 1798 rebellion and the United Irishmen is unclear. Certainly the Fenians and the United Irishmen shared a belief in the separation of Ireland from England and in the use of armed force to achieve that aim. Later, the leading Fenian John Devoy wrote that the ninety eight movement had left a spirit which had influenced the whole course of events in nineteenth century Ireland.[64] From the evidence of Fenian speeches and correspondence in the 1860s and 1870s, however, there is not much evidence that 1798 had much direct bearing on their ideas and actions.[65] In the speeches of Fenians from the dock, for example, there are few references to the men or events of 1798.[66] Rather, Fenian views on Irish nationality were influenced considerably by Thomas Davis while their arguments about physical force owed much to the writings of John Mitchel.[67] Fenianism was essentially a separatist, but not a doctrinaire republican, movement.[68]

Mainstream party politics in Ireland in the 1870s and 1880s contained few references to the 1798 rebellion or the United Irishmen. Speeches of delegates to the home rule conference in Dublin in November 1873 contain frequent mention of the past but this mostly relates to the constitution of 1782 and the example of the Irish Volunteers.[69] The Rev. Isaac Nelson, a presbyterian minister from Belfast, in a reference to 1798, spoke approvingly of five Belfast presbyterians who 'standing on the Cave Hill, clutched hands together, and vowed before heaven to devote their lives to their country's freedom', but his speech was an exception.[70] In his biography of C.S. Parnell, T.P. O'Connor claimed that stories about 1798 relating to County Wicklow had influenced C.S. Parnell, while in an other biography R. Barry O'Brien remarked that Parnell 'had certainly heard [something] of the rebellion of 1798 from the peasants in the [County Wicklow] neighbourhood, but the effect of these stories was transient'.[71] There were few references to 1798 in the speeches of either politicians or land reformers during the period, although when Michael Davitt was imprisoned during the Land War in 1882 his reading in jail included Wolfe Tone's memoirs as well as a life of O'Connell.[72]

While politics in Ulster during these decades were little influenced by what had happened in 1798, the rebellion had not been forgotten entirely, as Thomas MacKnight, editor of the Belfast liberal newspaper *The Northern Whig*, recalled in his memoirs, published in 1896. Describing political life in the late 1860s, he observed that:

The protestant liberals of Ulster, whose fathers and grandfathers were United Irishmen, had generally become warm supporters of the liberal party as it had been led by Charles Grey, Lord Melbourne, Lord John Russell and recently by Lord Palmerston. Though the descendants of the United Irishmen, they were not at all disposed themselves to become rebels; but they were rather proud than otherwise of their ancestors for having been rebels. The events of that time, two years before the Act of Union, were vividly present to the descendants of

those who had suffered in that dreadful resurrection, or series of resur-
rections. The wounds, though healed, left scars still visible. The scenes
of the battles, as at Ballynahinch, and of the executions, as of
McCracken in Belfast, were still pointed out.[73]

In the speeches of Ulster liberals and conservatives during the
decades up to 1885, and of unionists after that date, the 1798 rebellion was not a matter of reference. Most protestant liberals rejected
Gladstone's leadership when he took up home rule and they became
liberal unionists. Thomas MacKnight records that when a leading
English Gladstonian liberal in 1887 asked some liberal unionists to
explain why their position had apparently changed from a century
earlier, he was told that 'the liberties for which our fathers fought
and died have nearly all been conceded'.[74] Among northern nationalists, the 1798 rebellion does not seem to have been a matter of
great concern. We may note, however, that in the 1870s banners at
home rule parades in Derry and Downpatrick depicted United
Irishmen such as William Orr and Robert Emmet, alongside Pope
Pius IX and Daniel O'Connell.[75] Banners of the Irish National
Foresters, founded in the late 1870s, carried images of a wide range
of Irish historical figures, including heroes of 1798 and 1803.

During the period 1848–98 books continued to appear on the
subject of the 1798 rebellion. Publication of a second edition of
R.R. Madden's *History of the United Irishmen* commenced in 1858.
Madden took the opportunity to write new introductions to his
volumes in order to which reflect some of his current concerns. In
one he argued that the events of 1798 showed both the dangers of
misrule by government and the folly of people entering into secret
associations against oppression: in another he wrote an extensive
denunciation of Orangeism during and since the rebellion.[76] W.J.
Fitzpatrick, in his popular book *The Sham Squire; and the informers
of 1798*, which was first published in 1864, revealed information on
the network of government spies which had undermined the
United Irishmen's organisation. In a preface to the third edition,
published two years later, Fitzpatrick insisted that the rebellion had
been provoked by bad government and added that 'the policy of the

present government presents a thorough contrast to that of their remote predecessors, and in my opinion merits support'.[77] He also stated his disapproval of secret organisations. In 1874 the first edition appeared of Father Patrick Kavanagh's *Popular history of the insurrection of 1798*. Reprinted several times in the following decades, Father Kavanagh was concerned to minimise the fact that the United Irishmen were a secret organization. He dealt in particular with the rising in Wexford which he depicted as an alliance of catholic clergy and people against oppression. In a new introduction to the second edition in 1874 Kavanagh expressed his hope that 'our onward journey towards long lost liberty may be made by peaceful paths'.[78] All three writers, Madden, Fitzpatrick and Kavanagh, were enthusiastic supporters of the United Irishmen but they shared a dislike for secret organisations, a matter no doubt related to the contemporary issue of the secret I.R.B. to which they were all obviously hostile.

A different view of the United Irishmen and their relevance appeared in a pamphlet first published in 1867 called *Speeches from the dock, or protests of Irish freedom*. This publication brought together dock speeches by United Irishmen in 1798 and 1803, Young Irelanders in 1848 and Fenians in the 1860s. The introduction stated that 'it is by example that the great lessons of patriotism can best be conveyed'. For virtually the first time all these political figures were brought together to create an 'unbroken succession of political martyrs.'[79] In the speeches of Young Irelanders and Fenians reported here there are in fact very few references to the United Irishmen, but in this volume, which was republished many times, they were all linked together very clearly. The first figure in the volume was Theobald Wolfe Tone, although his declaration of August 1796, about breaking the link with England and substituting the name of Irishman in place of the different denominations, is not quoted here. Other accounts and editions of his writings in this period helped to give additional importance to Tone.[80] An American visitor to Tone's grave in 1861 had noted how since 1848 few visitors had come to Bodenstown: 'the ground beneath the tombstone was dry, hard and bare; and, judging from the feathers scattered around it, had apparently become a favourite resort for domestic fowl'. During the 1860s, however, due to these new publications and the advent of Fenianism, it seems there were growing numbers of visitors to Tone's grave. In 1873 a new memorial stone was erected by a Dublin based band called Wolfe Tone to replace the earlier Young Irelanders' memorial which had been broken.[81] Special pilgrimages to Bodenstown, on or near 20 June (the date of Tone's birth), seem to have begun on a regular annual basis only in 1891, but press reports show that by the mid 1890s these commemorations were attracting large numbers of people.[82]

The fifty years between 1848 and 1898 also saw the appearance of a number of works from the north which dealt with the rebellion. In 1853 a new impression of McSkimin's account was published in Belfast, under the title of *History of the Irish rebellion in the year 1798*. In 1857 the *Ballymena Observer* published a series of articles on the rebellion as it happened in the town and neighbourhood, and these were reprinted later in a separate volume, *Old Ballymena – a history of Ballymena during the 1798 rebellion...* (Ballymena, n.d.). McComb's *Guide to Belfast and the adjacent districts of the counties of Antrim and Down* (Belfast,1861), contained an extensive account of the Battle of Ballynahinch. A selection of material relating to the north from R.R. Madden's multi-volume history was published in a popular paperback version, entitled *Antrim and Down in '98* (Glasgow, n.d.). The year 1888 saw the appearance of a biography of Betsy Gray by W.G. Lyttle, called *Betsy Gray, or hearts of Down* (Bangor).[83] In the early 1890s the *Ulster Journal of Archaeology* published a series of articles on reminiscences of the rebellion which were reproduced in a Belfast printed volume in 1895, edited by Rev. W. J. Smith, entitled *Memories of '98*. R. M. Young was responsible for *Ulster episodes and anecdotes in '98* (Belfast, 1893) and for a short monograph on Mary Ann McCracken in his *Historical notices of old Belfast* (Belfast, 1896). In 1897 W. T. Latimer produced 1897 his *Ulster biographies* (Belfast) which covered a number of people involved in 1798. Alice Milligan commenced publication in Belfast in 1895 of her magazine *The Shan Van Vocht*, while her *Life of Theobald Wolfe Tone* was printed in Belfast in 1898.

Until the centenary celebrations for the 1798 rebellion in the late 1890s, the second half of the nineteenth century witnessed little in the way of public commemorations for 1798. The earliest known monument to the insurgents of 1798 was erected in St Mary's cemetery, Newtownbarry, now Bunclody, in County Wexford in 1875.[84] In 1876 nationalists in County Mayo dedicated a '98 monument in the form of a Celtic cross at French Hill outside Castlebar.[85] A number of men from County Wexford established a '98 club in Dublin and were responsible for the erection in 1878 of a memorial cross to the insurgents of 1798 at Boolavogue, County Wexford.[86] Support for these commemorations was limited and indeed in the case of the Boolavogue memorial there was a dispute between the '98 club and the local parish priest over its location. In 1888, in the preface to *Betsy Gray, or, hearts of Down,* the author W.G. Lyttle called for a monument to be raised by public subscription at the grave of '98 heroine Betsy Gray at Ballycreen, County Down. No support was forthcoming, however, and when a memorial was erected on her grave in 1896 it was paid for by her grandnephew.[87] In the 1880s emigrants from County Wexford formed '98 clubs in New York in order to plan commemorative events but these made little impact. By 1895, however, a number of prominent Irish-Americans had set up a '98 centennial association.[88] The Young Ireland League, founded in 1891, held a commemoration of the Battle of Vinegar Hill in May 1894.[89] More importantly, in 1897 the Young Ireland League ran a series of meetings to establish a '98 centenary committee in Dublin to direct the centenary celebrations.[90]

In contrast to the lack of public interest shown in 1798 and the United Irishmen in the decades immediately before 1898, the centenary was the occasion for widespread popular commemoration. As one recent commentator, however, has remarked: 'It is clear that the 1898 commemorations were motivated as much by contemporary political concerns as they were by the desire to memorialise the 1798 uprising'.[91] Following the Parnellite split, the 1890s had been a time of disillusionment and division in Irish nationalist politics.

One response to this was a growing interest in the past. In a speech to a '98 centenary meeting in February 1898, W.B. Yeats observed that 'Ireland was appealing to the past to escape the confusion of the present.'[92] The year 1897 had marked the diamond jubilee of Queen Victoria which had been keenly and widely celebrated in Ireland and many nationalists saw the centenary as an opportunity to encourage enthusiasm among members of nationalist Ireland. W. Allen, a member of the I.R.B. and a leading member of the Dublin based centennial executive, privately expressed his hope in December 1897 that the celebrations about 1798 might 'put a little national spirit into the young men here, and Lord knows they want it'.[93] For contemporary political rivals, the centenary also 'provided a new theatre in which they could verbally attack their opponents'.[94] The centennial executive was controlled initially by members of the I.R.B., who sought to exclude members of the divided parliamentary nationalist party, in particular the majority Anti-Parnellite wing, from its deliberations. John Dillon, leader of the Anti-Parnellite grouping, set up his own centenary organisation, but by May 1898 the centennial executive council had been restructured to allow Dillon's supporters to join it, although rivalry still continued between the different groups. [95] Throughout the country a large number of '98 associations, some independent and others linked to the main wings of the parliamentary party or, more rarely, the I.R.B., were formed.

In spite of these divisions, however, as Timothy O'Keefe has remarked, 'the centennial itself provided nationalist Ireland with a number of public demonstrations, continual newspaper coverage, and endless platform rhetoric'.[96] In many parts of Ireland efforts were made to erect monuments to commemorate 1798 and the United Irishmen. The names of streets in a number of towns were changed to honour '98 heroes. The principal event of the year was a large parade in Dublin on 15 August 1898 to mark the laying of the foundation stone for a memorial to Wolfe Tone.[97] An enormous crowd assembled in Dublin to watch the parade bring the stone, hewn from rocks at McArt's Fort in Belfast, location of an important meeting of United Irishmen in 1795, on a route which

passed important 1798 sites. At the final stone-laying ceremony in St Stephen's Green, spokesmen from a wide range of nationalist and republican backgrounds made impassioned speeches about Tone and modern day Ireland. This event marked a new level of recognition for Tone, although we may note the observation about him in the editorial of the *Freeman's Journal* on 15 August 1898:

> Some day perhaps, when a great and competent eulogist arises, the Irish people will begin to understand what Wolfe Tone has been to them. At present he is merely one of the striking figures in that marvellous epoch which began with 1780, and ended, twenty three-years later, with the execution of Robert Emmet.

It has been reckoned that forty monuments to United Irishmen and the events of 1798 were erected as a result of activities begun in this centenary year, although in many cases the actual monuments appeared some time after 1898, due to problems of fundraising.[98] In the case of the Wolfe Tone statue, it was not erected until 1967, after decades of infighting and financial incompetence by the organising committee.

From a reading of speeches, lectures and articles produced during 1898 we can see how different groups sought to use the centenary of 1798 as an opportunity to emphasise their commitment to nationalism and also to sometimes remind their audiences of their differences in approach. Constitutional nationalists were happy to claim identity with the United Irishmen, and stressed how they had resorted to violence only as a result of oppression. A the same time they also made clear that in the changed political climate Irish freedom could be achieved under their parliamentary leadership. John Redmond, M.P., declared that: 'The blood of the martyrs was not shed in vain. The efforts and sacrifices of the men of '98, '65, and '67 have borne fruit.' He continued: 'The statesmanship of Parnell not only achieved much, but will yet inspire the whole Irish nation to brave and wise deeds for its liberation.'[99] Republicans emphasised Tone's call for independence, attacked contemporaries for being 'soft' and spelt out links between 1798, 1849, 1867 and the present. At the laying of the foundation stone for the Tone statue in

Dublin, the Fenian veteran John O'Leary (who had previously placed a bust at Tone's grave at the June commemoration at Bodenstown) made the connection between 1798 and the Fenians by reminding people of his time in jail for Fenian activities.[100] Occasionally speakers in the various camps referred to the fact that Tone and other United Irishmen had been protestants and they urged the unity of all creeds and classes. The main call for unity at meetings, however, was for the unity of the different branches of nationalism.[101] Another feature sometimes found in centenary celebrations was the presentation of events and people of 1798 in a catholic 'faith and fatherland' context. In a speech at the laying of the foundation stone of the Wexford 1798 monument Father Patrick Kavanagh stated: 'This monument will be a proof to future generations that we were imbued with the spirit of the men of '98, and more, that we did not forget to worthily commemorate their fearless stand for faith and fatherland.'[102]

Northern responses to the centenary celebrations differed sharply between unionists and nationalists. During 1897 and 1898, a number of '98 clubs were formed. Reflecting nationalist rivalry elsewhere, the leadership and direction of these clubs became a matter of controversy which was resolved finally by the supremacy of the Dillon wing of the nationalist party, led in the north by Joseph Devlin. To promote and coordinate '98 activities he established in late 1897 an Ulster '98 central council, opposed to the I.R.B. dominated Dublin centennial executive council, and this body under his presidency became a leading part of the new country-wide organisation set up by John Dillon to rival the Dublin council.[103] A highlight of the northern celebrations was a parade on 6 June 1898 to mark the anniversary of the battle of Antrim. Consisting of around two dozen clubs and societies, drawn primarily from west Belfast, but also from Counties Down and Antrim, the parade marched from Smithfield Square in Belfast to a meeting place at Hannahstown on the western edge of the city. The first speaker was Devlin who declared that they 'were rebels in heart and they would be rebels in reality if they had the chance'. In several speeches the role of protestants in the ranks of the United Irishmen was acknowledged, but at the same time the demonstration was viewed clearly as a contemporary declaration by Belfast nationalists that, in John Dillon's words, 'the old spirit of Irish nationality, which has survived persecution and the proscriptions of four centuries is still today alive and kicking in Belfast, and is as ready for a fight as ever it was in the past'.[104] On the return journey from Hannahstown, the parade ran into opposition from loyalist and Orange protesters and serious rioting ensued, mainly between the police and protestant rioters. At the Wolfe Tone stone-laying ceremony in Dublin, a large contingent of northern '98 clubs was present, especially from Belfast. Other '98 activities in Ulster during the year included a concert in Newry in honour of the United Irishmen and trips by '98 clubs to the site of the battle of Ballynahinch.[105]

Among the unionist and protestant population in the north there was little enthusiasm for the 1798 centenary celebrations. The presbyterian general assembly met in Belfast during the week of the anniversary of the battle of Antrim but there was no mention of the event or of the Hannahstown demonstration and subsequent riots in its deliberations.[106] In part this lack of interest was due to the qualms of those who were worried about protestants suffering in 1798 and of others who were concerned about manifestations of 'faith and fatherland' in the contemporary celebrations of 1798. A statement from the Belfast Grand Orange Lodge on the eve of the Hannahstown demonstration referred to the persecution of protestants in 1798.[107] Reports in the *Belfast News Letter,* the *Northern Whig* and the *Irish Times* drew attention to the fact that the day chosen for the laying of the foundation stone for Wolfe Tone's monument was the catholic holiday of 15 August, Lady's day.[108] The principal reservations, however, arose because the anniversary was seen as dominated by nationalist groups who regarded the historical celebrations as an opportunity to promote Irish nationalism. After the Hannahstown demonstration, the *Northern Whig* declared that 'the demonstration was well understood to have... not a historical but a prospective application.' It continued: 'The centenary celebrations are avowedly for the establishment of an independent Irish nationalist government.'[109] The paper reported Devlin's remark at Hannahstown that: 'As in 1798, the men of today were rebels in heart, and those feelings would never be eradicated from their breasts until every vestige of British rule was swept out of the country.'[110] A small number of protestants, such as Alice Milligan, were nationalist in sympathy and they had some involvement in these celebrations, but even for them the centenary was seen primarily as an opportunity to assert nationalist or republican aims. Writing in 1898 about Wolfe Tone, Alice Milligan acknowledged the dangers of sectarianism and disunity, but insisted that Tone's 'aim was not unity, but freedom'.[111]

The alienation of protestants from these celebrations is illustrated most vividly in the destruction of the memorial stone to Betsy Gray. After the erection of the memorial in 1896 her grave became a popular spot for visitors. In April 1898 plans were announced for a number of nationalist groups, both local and from further afield, to hold a demonstration at the graveside on Sunday, 1 May.[112] Several wreaths were laid on her grave beforehand, including one which carried lines from a poem calling for 'God's wrath upon the Saxon'. A large party of local protestants assembled, however, and destroyed the memorial before the arrival of the nationalists. James Mills, who was present at this destruction, later described the event:

> There was to have been a special ceremony at the grave on that Sunday to mark the centenary of the '98 rising and local protestants were inflamed because it was being organised by Roman Catholics and other Home-Rulers. They didn't like these people claiming Betsy, and they became so enraged that they decided to prevent the ceremony from taking place, and they smashed the monument with sledgehammers.[113]

The centenary of the Battle of Ballynahinch on 13 June was marked by nationalist and loyalist parades in the town which passed off peacefully, although several weeks later the presence of a fifty strong police force was required to prevent trouble between opposing factions. Apart from the unionist parade to celebrate the loyalist victory at the battle of Ballynahinch, there were no pro-union parades, although at the 12th July celebrations events of 1798 were referred to in a number of platform speeches. The Rev. L.A. Pooler, in a speech at 12th July celebrations at Ballynahinch, declared:

> He was happy to say that every constitutional reform which the
> Volunteers desired, and every grievance of which the United men com-
> plained, had found a remedy long ago by a parliament of the United
> Kingdom. If an inhabitant of Ballynahinch in 1798 could stand there
> that day, he would see great changes. He could see signs of industry
> and prosperity all around; he could see the descendants of the United
> men in thousands praising God for the union and wearing Orange
> sashes.[114]

When George Bernard Shaw was asked in 1898 to 'help [his]
downtrodden countrymen by assembling with other Irishmen to
romance about 1798' he refused and declared that 'until Irishmen
apply themselves to what the condition of Ireland will be in 1998,
they will get very little patriotism out of yours sincerely'.[115] In fact
people were more interested in the Ireland of the future than in the
Ireland of the past. These bicentenary celebrations were very much
part of current arguments about the future not only between
unionists and nationalists, but between different forms of nationalists. With the passage of time people in the nationalist camp could
now forget or ignore the violence of 1798 and commemorate the
rebellion in light of their contemporary interests and concerns. The
events and people of 1798 could be enthusiastically presented in
such a way as to justify and strengthen nationalist perspectives and
objectives. This historical dimension was used to provide a series of
heroes and events which seemed to bolster historical arguments for
modern day nationalists, especially of the home rule constitutional
variety. The strong sense of nationalism engendered by these events
encouraged constitutional nationalists to be concerned about the
divisions in their ranks and this led to the reunification of the parliamentary party in 1900 under John Redmond.[116] For some revolutionary nationalists the centenary also proved inspirational,
although this would have little direct political effect for another
decade. Unionists also responded to the bicentenary, according
to their contemporary needs, by largely ignoring the occasion. It
cannot be said that unionists did not know about these events, but

rather that in the circumstances of the late nineteenth century, when they strongly backed the union, they did not wish to support an historical view which seemed to undermine their position. Furthermore, in light of the obvious nationalist and catholic dominance of the centenary and its associated events, most unionists and protestants, even descendants of the United Irishmen, felt unable to partake in the commemoration of 1798.

III

The period between the centenary celebrations and the outbreak of the first world war saw a waning of interest in 1798 and the United Irishmen. In 1903 there were commemorative events in honour of Robert Emmet and the 1803 rising.[117] While annual pilgrimages to Tone's grave at Bodenstown continued to take place on the Sunday closest to his birthday (20 June), the numbers involved seem to have been much lower than in the 1890s.[118] Around 1910 new railings were erected at his grave by the County Kildare Gaelic Association, but efforts to erect a statue in his honour in Dublin continued to meet with failure. In 1905 a statement from the Tone memorial committee admitted ruefully that after the Dublin demonstration of August 1898, 'the country deserted the movement'.[119] In 1911 supporters of Tone suffered the ignominy of seeing the unveiling in Dublin of both a statue of Parnell in O'Connell Street and also a memorial arch in honour of those Dubliners who died in the crown forces in the Boer War beside the site on St Stephen's Green originally selected for the Tone statue. This decline in interest in Tone may have been partly the consequence of allegations of incompetence and of financial irregularities concerning the Tone memorial committee.[120] In addition these years seem to have involved a general fall in concern about the revolutionary events and heroes of 1798. In his poem, 'September 1913', composed after the funeral of the Fenian John O'Leary as a protest against what he saw as contemporary inertia, W.B Yeats asked: 'Was it ... for this Edward Fitzgerald died. And Robert Emmet and Wolfe Tone'.[121]

Some work on 1798 was published during these years, but it consisted mainly of reprints such as Father Patrick Kavanagh's history
and McSkimin's account.[122] F.J. Bigger did write a biography of the
United Irishman, William Orr, which was to be the first of a series
of books on prominent northern figures in 1798, but this was the
only one to appear.[123] A popular literary form of celebration of the
United Irishmen in the early twentieth century was the writing and
production of a number of patriotic melodramas on the individuals and events of 1798.[124] The Queen's Royal Theatre in Dublin
was a popular venue for these works by writers such as J.W.
Whitbread and P.J. Bourke. The play *Cathleen ni Houlihan,* by
W.B. Yeats, first performed in 1902, was set in the west of Ireland
just prior to the rebellion of 1798. It has been calculated that
around thirty popular novels on the subject of the 1798 rebellion
were published between 1880 and 1914, over half between 1898
and 1914.[125] Contemporary newspapers and magazines often seri-
alized these works and so brought them to a wide audience. On 18
December 1920 the *Irish Weekly,* which claimed to have the largest
circulation for a weekly newspaper in Ireland, carried a lengthy
extract from M.T. Pender's *The ordeal of Bride Gilmurray,* described
as a thrilling story of 'The ninety eight'.[126] In the late nineteenth
and early twentieth centuries, the Glasgow publishers Cameron,
Ferguson produced cheap paperback editions of various histories on
people or events of 1798.

The years immediately after 1898 saw the completion of a number of projects, begun in that year, to erect memorials and statues
to the United Irishmen of 1798.[127] On 6 August 1905 Oliver
Sheppard's statue of a pikeman was unveiled at Wexford before a
very large crowd of people, not only locals but also people from
Dublin and Liverpool. Joseph McConnell of Wicklow county
council praised the work of the Irish parliamentary party and stated that 'Mr Redmond and his colleagues were waging a terrific fight
every day at Westminster against an enemy eight times their
strength, and was dealing the enemy blow for blow in a manner
characteristic for '98.'[128] In May 1908 another memorial by
Shepperd was unveiled at Enniscorthy, County Wexford. Clerical

speakers, including Father Patrick Kavanagh who performed the ceremony, reminded listeners of the close links between the catholic clergy and the people both in the present moment and also in 1798 'when they fought side-by-side for faith and fatherland.' William Redmond M.P., acknowledged the bravery and the aims of the United Irishmen: 'the Irish people are in no position to resort to arms but the spirit is there ... the aspirations of the patriots of '98 must be satisfied, and full measure of national freedom must be granted to Ireland.'[129] In September 1914 images of 1798 were recalled by John Redmond, as leader of the Irish parliamentary party, at Woodenbridge in Co. Wicklow in 1914, when he urged the Irish volunteers to join the allied war effort in Europe and emulate the bravery of the men of 1798.[130]

Clearly supporters of the constitutional Irish parliamentary party saw no problems in being involved in the commemorative events for the United Irishmen of 1798. Advocates of more revolutionary politics could also join in such commemorations for their own benefit, although we may note that in 1906 some members of Sinn Féin argued that the movement to put up 1798 monuments had been 'a mistaken policy' and a waste of energy, and what was required was more direct methods of obtaining the national goal.[131] In 1899, following the centenary celebration, Arthur Griffith founded the radical nationalist weekly paper, the *United Irishman*. In its first issue it declared that 'we accept the nationalism of '98, '49 and '67 as the true nationalism'.[132] In 1901 Griffith stated in the paper that: 'Grattan is dead and O'Connell is dead and Parnell is dead, but Emmet and Davis, Mitchel and the Fenian Men are living still'.[133] The paper ran until 1906 during which time Griffith put forward various radical proposals such as the idea that M.P.s should refuse to attend Westminster and instead meet in Dublin. Griffith, however, did not support an Irish republic and was opposed to armed insurrection. He accepted the constitution of 1782 and was willing to recognise the British king as head of an Irish parliament.[134] In 1905 Griffith founded Sinn Féin, which, while promoting various advanced political ideas and claiming links to the United Irishmen, also advocated the idea of two kingdoms under one crown. Failure at by-elections over the next few years, however, showed that at this stage Sinn Féin had little popular support compared to the major backing for the Irish parliamentary nationalist party and there was little encouragement for radical nationalism. In 1914, Sean MacDermott, addressing members of the I.R.B. in County Kerry, stated that: 'Nationalism as known to Tone and Emmet is almost dead in the country and a spurious substitute, as taught by the Irish parliamentary party, exists', He went on: 'The generation now growing old is the most decadent generation nationally since the Norman invasion, and the Irish patriotic spirit will die forever unless a blood sacrifice is made in the next few years.'[135]

In the north, in the years immediately after the centenary celebrations, there was little public interest in either the United Irishmen or the 1798 rebellion. No monuments or memorials were unveiled, in contrast to the rest of Ireland. The '98 clubs established at the centenary under the influence of Joseph Devlin did not survive long after the centenary, although members were probably integrated into the United Irish League or the Ancient Order of Hibernians, both of which became important nationalist and catholic organisations in Ulster under Devlin's control in the early 1900s. Building on the power base established during the centenary celebrations, Devlin successfully opposed the catholic bishop of Down and Connor, Dr Henry Henry, to become the main political voice for Belfast catholics and then in 1906 to be elected M.P. for West Belfast.[136] Devlin founded a newspaper, the *Northern Star*, called after the Belfast paper of the United Irishmen. In spite of its name, however, the *Northern Star* often carried openly anti-protestant articles.[137] Up to the first world war, the Irish parliamentary party dominated northern nationalist politics. Nonethless, some clubs of Na Fianna Éireann, a republican youth movement founded in 1909, were established in Belfast.[138] The *Irish News* of 26 June 1913 reported that 'for the first time within the memory of the present generation' a pilgrimage to McArt's Fort, Cavehill, was held to commemorate the birth of Wolfe Tone. Six clubs of Na Fianna Éireann (Neilsons, McCrackens, Betsy Grays, O'Neills, Orrs,

Tones) marched from the Falls Road to Cavehill, where an address was delivered and songs and recitations performed.

The lack of interest felt by unionists at this time in the subject of the United Irishmen was described by the nationalist Joseph Connolly in his memoirs. He recalled his thoughts walking around Donegall Square, Belfast, on the evening of Covenant Day, 28 September 1912, when most of the unionist community had signed a covenant to oppose home rule:

> The Belfast of 1798, of William Orr, of Jimmy Hope, of Henry Joy McCracken, of Neilson, Steele Dickson and all the other patriots was gone. There was no recollection of patriotic ministers and laymen who believed in freedom and who went to their deaths in their efforts to achieve it. ... The sturdy farmers who had been the mainstay of the Tenant-Right movement as well as the insurgents of 1782 and 1798 were repudiated and disowned by their descendants.[139]

It would be wrong to say that these events had been entirely forgotten by the unionist community. J.C. MacDermott, Lord Chief Justice of Northern Ireland from 1951 to 1971, described how in his youth in the early 1900s his family still recounted stories about 1798.[140] But for most unionists these events had no contemporary relevance and they were unwilling to celebrate them publicly. There were a few protestant nationalists in Ulster, however, who did maintain a strong interest in 1798. The Belfast antiquarian and local historian, F.J. Bigger, published material relating to the rebellion and was the centre of a small circle, including Sir Roger Casement, which were interested in the United Irishmen.[141] Some members of this group were involved in the cultural magazine *Uladh*.[142] Bulmer Hobson was another northern protestant with a strong interest in 1798. In his autobiography, he states how as a schoolboy during the '98 centenary celebrations he was inspired by Wolfe Tone and the United Irishmen.[143] Influenced by Arthur Griffith, Hobson inaugurated in 1905 the Dungannon clubs, named after the Irish volunteer movement of 1782. Later he became a supporter of an independent Irish republic, joined the I.R.B., helped to establish Na Fianna Éireann and in 1911 was made editor of the I.R.B. paper

Irish Freedom, with its motto from Tone 'to break the connection with England'.[144]

Although members of the I.R.B. had played an important part in the '98 centenary celebrations, the organisation failed to experience any significant growth in the following decade for its revolutionary role.[145] Only after 1912 when a number of younger members, particularly Bulmer Hobson and Patrick Pearse, began to take an active part, did it assume a more vital role in Irish politics. For Pearse, the example and writings of former revolutionaries became important.[146] He first admired Emmet and then was attracted to Tone. His reverence for Tone was stated clearly in a speech at the Bodenstown commemoration in June 1913. He described Tone as the greatest Irishman who had ever lived and quoted his lines about breaking the link with England and uniting the whole people of Ireland. Over the next three years, in a number of publications and speeches, while concerned also with Davis and Lalor, Pearse expounded in detail on Tone's ideas of nationality and revolution. His interpretation of Tone and the events of 1798 were a strong influence in his involvement in the Easter Rising in Dublin in 1916. The proclamation of the republic did not specifically mention 1798 but described how 'six times during the past three hundred years' the Irish people had asserted in arms 'their right to national freedom and sovereignty.'[147] Other leaders of the rising, such as James Connolly, were also influenced by 1798, especially Wolfe Tone. On hearing news of events in Dublin the first reaction of a northern unionist, Adam Duffin (a descendant of the United Irishman William Drennan), was to liken the rising to a 'comic opera founded on the Wolf [sic] Tone fiasco a hundred years ago'.[148] In 1916, shortly before his execution for his part in the rising, Sir Roger Casement wrote: 'I am not afraid to die, to join Wolfe Tone and Robert Emmet, and hope that my death may one day help to make our country free'.[149]

After 1916 these events of 1798 remained important for many in the growing republican community. The Sinn Féin manifesto on the eve of the 1918 general election referred indirectly to 1798 when it declared how 'five times within the past 120 years our people have challenged in arms the right of England to rule this country'.[150] For many of those involved in the War of Independence the revolutionary tradition, which included the United Irishmen, was an important influence. The republican Ernie O'Malley admired Tone as a man of action and acknowledged the impact of his writings on him in the period immediately after the rising: 'Delving amongst a heap of books which were in my study I found a first edition of Wolfe Tone's *Autobiography* in two volumes and this I read.'[151] For others the influence of 1798 may have been a more general one, through history books and folklore. A biographer of Michael Collins has stated that Collins's father heard tales of Tone from Diarmuid O' Suilleabhion who claimed to have been out in 1798 and fought with Tone, 'shoulder to shoulder', although Tone never actually fought in Ireland.[152] A British soldier who witnessed Kevin Barry's execution in November 1920 observed how quickly Barry had become part of a tradition going back to 1798:

> There was a man with a tray…. selling rosaries and other mementoes…he had a pile of cotton handkerchiefs bearing the semblance of young Kevin Barry surrounded by the portraits of former Irish heroes, Tone, Edward Fitzgerald, Emmet, Napper Tandy, Hamilton Rowan. My brother bought the handkerchief and hid it in a drawer.[153]

Due to the Easter Rising and consequent events, the public June pilgrimage to Tone's grave at Bodenstown did not occur again between 1916 and 1921. When this annual commemoration recommenced in 1922, however, the character of the occasion had changed markedly. First, thanks to the political success of followers of Tone, it attracted many of the leading politicians of the day. Secondly, reflecting the divisions within republicanism after the Treaty, rival organisations marked the day separately. On 23 June 1924, for example, the *Irish Independent* described how 'a national tribute to the memory of Wolfe Tone was paid yesterday at Bodenstown. President Cosgrave, the heads of the Irish army and judiciary and eight hundred Irish soldiers assembled to do honour to the great patriot.' Wreaths were laid at Tone's grave and W.T. Cosgrave gave an oration, after which the troops held a parade followed by a volley of shots and the sounding of the 'last post'. In the wake of the official demonstration, an anti-treaty party, consisting of contingents of Cumann na mBan and Sinn Féin clubs held a march to the grave, where a republican T.D., Brian O'Higgins, delivered a speech. In 1925 the official graveside oration was delivered by the minister of defence, who acknowledged Tone as the founding father of the Irish army, and from this time on it was the role of this minister, in the company of the president and other members of the executive council, to deliver the government address.[154] Also in 1925, Eamon de Valera, in the company of Pearse's mother and Countess Constance Markievicz, addressed the anti treaty pilgrimage for the first time. By 1927 numbers at the unofficial republican pilgrimage had grown considerably and now included representatives of Fianna Fáil.[155] Besides those involved in the two parades the event attracted large numbers of the general public.

On these occasions Tone was given great praise. At the same time speakers selected from Tone's life and writings according to their own political agendas. In his 1924 oration, for example, Cosgrave pointed to similarities between Tone and Michael Collins.[156] In 1926 republican J.A. Madden T.D. asserted that 'Tone had never deviated from the object of his life – complete separation from England and the establishment of an Irish republic.'[157] Sometimes speakers spoke of the need for unity. In 1925, for example, de Valera declared that; 'the republican basis was the only possible one on which they could be united.'[158] Very rarely, however, did any speech refer to the need for unity of protestant and catholic. In 1924 Cosgrave lauded Tone's attempt to substitute the name of Irishman for the labels of protestant, catholic and dissenter, but such sentiment does not seem to have been repeated by speakers at Bodenstown during the 1920s.[159] Partition was seldom referred to at length in these Bodenstown speeches. In 1926 the National Graves Association was established as a permanent body to oversee the upkeep of patriot graves and monuments, including a number of '98 memorials. Efforts to raise sufficient funds to erect the Tone memorial continued to meet with failure and matters fell to a new low in the 1920s when a treasurer of the memorial committee was charged with embezzlement.

Differences of opinion about the contemporary relevance of the 1798 rebellion were also revealed in September 1928 at Ballinamuck, County Longford, at the unveiling of a memorial to mark the 130th anniversary of the battle of Ballinamuck.[160] Father John Keville, a local parish priest, used the occasion to praise the Free State. He stated that the battle of Ballinamuck 'was fought in defence of faith and fatherland... to retrieve a lost cause – lost in 1798, but triumphant in 1928'. When M.J. Kennedy, a Fianna Fáil T.D., urged those present to renew their 'republican pledges', Keville ordered him to sit down. Kennedy complained how at such events the clergy ensured that the word 'republican' was banned 'even when commemorating the memory of the greatest republicans in Irish history'. Lord Longford, also spoke from the platform, and indeed made the most republican speech of all. A descendant of one of the British army staff officers at the original battle, Longford took the opportunity to show his strong sympathies for Wolfe Tone and the rebels of 1798: 'In honouring the memory of those who died, let us take a lesson from their sacrifice. They were not afraid to give up all for their country and it is for us to use every effort to make it a great nation. Dia Saor Éire'.

During the 1920s little was published on the personalities or events of 1798, apart from Bulmer Hobson's life of Tone, consisting of extracts from Tone's writings.[161] In the 1930s, however, there was a steady stream of material. In 1933 H.M. Hyde challenged the normally hostile picture of Lord Castlereagh, chief secretary of Ireland during the rebellion, while in 1937 Rosamund Jacob produced her study of the rise of the United Irishmen.[162] The bulk of writing, however, concentrated on Wolfe Tone. In 1932 the former T.D. Brian O'Higgins began publication of the *Wolfe Tone Annual* which ran for three decades. Criticism arose in some catholic circles that, because of his personal life and his criticism of the papacy, Tone was unsuitable as a founding figure of Irish nationalism.[163] There was considerable debate in the press on the matter in the thirties. In his book, *Wolfe Tone and the United Irishmen: for or against Christ?* published in 1937, the clerical student, Leo McCabe strongly denounced Tone.[164] In 1936 the northern protestant nationalist, Denis Ireland, published his selection of Tone's writings under the title *Patriot adventurer.*[165] In 1937 Sean O'Faolain abridged and edited Tone's autobiography, for the first time including for some of the material excised by Tone's son.[166] Frank MacDermot's study of Tone and his times appeared in 1939. An admirer of Tone and appointed to the senate by Eamon de Valera, MacDermot, nonetheless, was prepared to acknowledge Tone's share of the blame for the violence which accompanied the rebellion and which left the country bitterly divided.[167]

The 1930s began with increased emphasis on the Bodenstown event in June by both government and non-government sides. In 1930 the official commemoration included a fly-past by the Irish air force.[168] The next year the unofficial parade included not only a Fianna Fáil party but also a large contingent of I.R.A. members.[169] In response to this I.R.A. turnout led by Sean McBride, the government attempted but failed to prevent the use of military orders and marching by republicans. The following year, 1932, after the election of the Fianna Fáil government, saw neither government nor Fianna Fáil representation at the June Bodenstown commemorations.[170] In 1933, however, the minister for defence held an official parade on the morning of 25 June, while in the afternoon there was a Fianna Fáil parade, led by de Valera, to the graveside. A week earlier there had been an unofficial parade attended by forty-five I.R.A. units, accompanied for the first time by members of the newly formed Irish communist party.[171] In 1934 there was a similar schedule with parades on different days. The republican parade now included members of the break away socialist group, the Republican Congress.[172] By 1935 the Bodenstown parade had become a massive display of I.R.A. strength with a large number of units from all over Ireland on parade, along with thousands of supporters.[173]

By 1936, however, the government had declared the I.R.A. an illegal organisation and steps were now taken to prevent I.R.A. participation at the Tone event in June. The *Irish Independent,* 22 June

1936, declared that 'Bodenstown yesterday was an armed camp'. It described how 'about 1000 troops, with full army equipment, and supported by aeroplanes, were quartered in the vicinity of the cemetery... and about 500 gardai were also on duty'. Only a small number of republicans took part in the Tone pilgrimage that year. In the next two years both official and republican parades occurred but with relatively small numbers of supporters. In 1939, however, because of an upsurge in I.R.A. activity, the government banned the June Bodenstown commemorations and stationed troops and gardai at the graveyard to ensure that they did not take place; they were successful in their efforts although there were protests and disorder in both Dublin and County Cork over the ban. In June 1938 the 140th anniversary of the 1798 was marked by a number of commemorative events, mainly in County Wexford, culminating on 26 June at Vinegar Hill with a large procession and ceremony, which involved a reported twenty thousand people from all over Ireland.[174]

In the speeches by spokesmen from the various parties at Bodenstown during the 1930s tribute was paid to Tone in different ways. At the government commemorations, the main speaker continued to be the minister of defence, whether Cumann na Gaedheal or Fianna Fáil, and he usually stressed the value of the example of Tone for the state's armed forces. Republicans frequently quoted Tone's objective of breaking the connection with England and often attacked the Irish and British governments. In 1932, Sean Russell, the I.R.A. leader, declared that 'Tone's ideals have not yet been realised'. He continued: 'We have two regiments of the British army – one dressed in khaki in the north and the other dressed in green in the south – and a representative of the English King in both places'.[175] Many speakers, on all sides, used Tone's name to call for unity, but this usually meant the unity of nationalists or republicans, and partition was not commonly raised in platform speeches. In 1933 one speaker talked of union 'with all who take pride in being Irish in this outpost of the Gael', while another spoke of the need for union 'after years of fratricidal strife'.[176]

Press reports from the 1930s reveal that reference to Tone's idea of uniting 'protestant, catholic and dissenter' was largely absent from Bodenstown speeches. In 1930, however, we may note an oblique reference to this matter by Eamon de Valera.[177] He acknowledged that differences of religion and tradition made national unity difficult and he stated that they should be as sensitive to the rights of other Irishmen as to their own. In 1933, Maurice Twomey, chief of staff of the I.R.A., declared that republicans honoured the words of the proclamation of the republic which guaranteed religious freedom to all citizens.[178] In the rest of his speech, however, he never referred to protestants but dwelt at length on denying accusations that the I.R.A. was against the catholic church. In 1934 the republican parade actually included men from Orange areas of Belfast, including the Shankill Road, who were members of the Republican Congress. Fighting broke out, however, when they refused to lower their flags on republican orders and they were then forcibly prevented by republicans from getting to Tone's graveside. The following day the *Irish Times* commented on the irony of Ulster protestants being prevented by Tipperary catholics from honouring Wolfe Tone.[179] In 1938 the republican Michael Conway, in a rare reference to the matter, declared that 'as disciples of Tone they stood for unity among all Irishmen, irrespective of creed or class' and if they succeeded in uniting the people of Ireland, there would be an end to partition.[180]

During the second world war there seems to have been no public commemoration of Tone at Bodenstown, but the event recommenced in 1946. In 1948 at the 150th anniversary of the 1798, events and personalities of the rebellion were commemorated extensively in many parts of Ireland. To mark this anniversary, there were celebrations and parades from early June to September, organised by the All-Ireland '98 Commemoration Association.[181] Nearly every weekend during this period there were activities organized on the subject of 1798. In the early part of these celebrations, attention focussed on Wexford, Wicklow and Carlow, while later in the year there were events in the west, in particular at Killaloe and Castlebar. Often the commemorations were colourful occasions, involving pageants and historical reenactments, such as the reconstruction, involving units of the Irish army, on 1 August 1948 of the 'Castlebar races' of 1798.[182] Leading politicians from both the inter-party government and the opposition parties played a prominent part in the celebrations.

Speeches at these events concentrated on various themes. The bravery and sacrifice of those who fought in 1798 was dwelt upon. At the same time speakers emphasised the legacy of these events and heroes in the present. In contrast to the speeches at Bodenstown in the 1920s and 1930s there was frequent reference to the north, and partition was often denounced. On 11 July 1948 Father Patrick Murphy, chairman of the All Ireland '98 Commemoration Association, stated:

> We would like that these celebrations would result in the linking up of our organisation with the fight for the abolition of partition as the aims and objects of the men who died in '98 will not have been achieved, as long as England holds the lands of the O'Donnells and the O'Neills.[183]

At an event in County Wicklow on 22 August 1948, President Sean O'Kelly, William Norton (labour), Sean McBride (Clann na Poblachta), and Eamon de Valera (Fianna Fáil), all demanded an end to partition.[184] Speeches at these '98 celebrations often referred to 'alien rule' or the role of the British army in the north as the cause of partition.[185] Occasionally, however, as in several speeches of the taoiseach, John Costello, there were references to the role of protestants in the ranks of United Irishmen in 1798 and also an appeal to northern protestants to co-operate with the south to end partition.[186]

In the north plans were also made to celebrate the 150th anniversary of 1798. In August 1948 a local Belfast '98 committee announced a number of events for Belfast, including a major rally on 13 September, to be followed by a ceili in the Ulster Hall. A few days before the rally, the minister of home affairs, Edmund Warnock, announced a ban on the rally parading through central Belfast and restricted it to the west of the city.[187] Plans to hold the ceili in the Ulster Hall were jeopardised when Belfast city corporation withdrew its permission for the event on the grounds that it could lead to a breach of the peace. An injunction, however, was taken against the corporation's actions and the lord chief justice, Sir James Andrews, ordered that the ceili be allowed to proceed. He declared that 'those who observe the law are entitled to have their legal rights recognised and protected by the law as administered in the King's Court'.[188] A rally of around 15,000 persons took place on 19 September in nationalist areas of Belfast and the ceili was held in the Ulster hall. These commemorations of 1798 were seen as strongly political by both supporters and opponents. Cal McCrystal, son of Cathal McCrystal, chairman of the Belfast '98 commemoration association, later recalled the scene in Belfast:

> Belfast was flooded with pro-nationalist propaganda: elegies to Wolfe Tone and long dead hunger-strikers, such as Terence MacSwiney, a former Mayor of Cork. A 'Wolfe Tone commemoration' booklet had a garish front cover, depicting an Irish soldier standing on the British union flag and hoisting the Irish tricolour. It devoted a full page to MacSwiney's poem, 'A call to arms', and carried articles that encouraged youth to 'march down freedom's road'.[189]

In these commemorations in Belfast, acknowledgement was paid to the role of protestants, such as Jemmy Hope and Henry Joy McCracken, in the '98 rebellion, but few protestants or unionists seem to have been involved directly in the 1948 events in the city. Gusty Spence, the former U.V.F. leader, recalled being brought to the Belfast parade by a catholic friend: 'He took me to a parade on the Falls in 1948, marking the 150th anniversary of the 1798 rising, and for the first time I heard that all the rebels in Belfast were protestants. We were taught no Irish history, so it was very confusing.'[190] Some unionists, however, did have an indirect involvement in these affairs. Edmund Warnock, who banned the '98 parade from central Belfast, was the descendant of a County Antrim United Irishman. Sir James Andrews, lord chief justice and brother of J.M. Andrews, former prime minister of Northern Ireland, who upheld the right of the '98 committee to hold their ceili, was descended from William Drennan, one of the founders of the

United Irishmen. Jack Loudan's *Henry Joy McCracken*, was produced at the Group Theatre in Belfast in the spring of 1948, while shortly afterwards John Hewitt wrote *The McCrackens*, although this was not performed until 1998.[191]

The 1948 commemorations for the 1798 rebellion reflected a new level of nationalist celebrations, compared with 1898. Those involved included the leading members of the southern government and opposition parties who used the events to demonstrate their concern for heightened contemporary concerns about partition and republican goals. The attention paid to the north, which had been rarely shown in '98 commemorations at Bodenstown in the 1920s and 1930s, reflected the influence of the newly formed Clann na Poblachta party and the response of other parties to it. The inter-party government passed the Republic of Ireland Act in late 1948, an action which may have been encouraged by the enthusiastic republicanism of the '98 celebrations during that year. In Northern Ireland those involved in the commemorations for the 1798 rebellion came almost entirely from the nationalist or republican communities. Reflecting how this historical event was still seen in contemporary unionist v nationalist terms, members of the unionist and protestant communities either ignored or sought to curtail public celebration of the event.

IV

After the widespread and popular celebrations in 1948 for the 150th anniversary of the rebellion, the main focus for '98 commemorations returned to the annual June Bodenstown pilgrimage, marked separately by an army ceremony led by the minister of defence, a Fianna Fáil tribute and a republican parade, including various organisations. From 1949 to 1955 the national press carried reasonable coverage of Bodenstown but from 1956 to 1965 accounts of these events were usually brief and rarely carried reports of any of the speeches. In 1964, in honour of the bicentenary of Wolfe Tone's birth, two postage stamps were issued, although this was belated, occurring a year after the bicentenary date and only after complaints that his anniversary had been ignored. The stamps carried simply a portrait of Tone, in contrast to stamps issued in 1948 which showed not just his portrait but also pictures of a pikeman and French ships.[192] Other '98 events occurred during this period. In June 1956 a six and a half foot sculptured Celtic cross was erected at the Montmartre Cemetery in Paris in honour of the 1798 insurgent and French soldier, Myles Byrne.[193] On 19 June 1960 a plaque was unveiled at Ballinglen, County Wicklow, by the taoiseach Sean Lemass, to mark the place where two insurgents, Patrick and Philip Lacey, were shot in 1798. Lemass declared that the numerous monuments and memorials throughout the country testified to the courage with which the Irish people had fought for their freedom. He then stated his belief that 'the historic task of this generation of Irishmen [is] to build unshakeable and indestructible economic foundations for our political freedom.' He believed that when this was achieved other national aims would meet with success: a higher level of Irish economic attainment would help to clear away one of the continuing arguments used to justify partition.[194]

In November 1967, nearly seven decades after the great parade of August 1898, the statue of Wolfe Tone was finally erected. It was situated on St Stephen's Green at the north-east corner and not, as originally planned, at the Grafton Street corner, where a monument to Dublin soldiers who had served in the British army in the Boer War, now stood. The original foundation stone, hewn out of rock from McArt's Fort in Belfast was not used. After remaining in its original position on St Stephen's Green for a brief time, the stone had been removed as a traffic hazard and stored for many years in a Dublin corporation yard before being placed in the city hall; it was then put in the graveyard at St Mary's church in Dublin, where Tone had been baptised.[195] After falling into abeyance, the idea of the Tone memorial had been raised again in the late 1950s by Mrs Kathleen Clarke, widow of the 1916 leader Tom Clarke. The Irish Arts Council became involved in the project and, with government financial backing, the sculptor Edward Delaney was commissioned to design the statue.[196] On Saturday 18 November 1967 Tone's memorial was unveiled by President Eamon de Valera, in the presence of Tone's descendants, Church of Ireland archbishop of Dublin, G.O. Simms, the taoiseach, Jack Lynch, other members of the government and some veterans of 1916.

In his speech de Valera said how they had raised 'in this part of the country, the republic [Tone] longed for and worked for'. He continued:

> It would, of course, sorrow Tone's heart not to have the whole nation united and there are not here today representatives from Belfast of the presbyterians, those people whom he regarded as the most freedom loving and liberty loving of the whole of our people. Their absence today would sorrow him a great deal, but let us have the hope and courage that Wolfe Tone had. Let us work to see that this ultimate ideal will be realised.[197]

He urged people to read Tone's published work. The presence of de Valera and government ministers at this event served to mark the official significance given to Tone. At the same time there were small numbers at the unveiling, compared to the large crowds in 1898, and there was no military parade. On the Monday following the unveiling, the *Irish Independent* and the *Irish Times* gave the occasion moderate coverage in their inside pages, while the *Irish Press* ignored it but reported on other commemorative events over the weekend, such as the Manchester Martyrs' memorial ceremony in Cork, the 1920 Bloody Sunday commemoration in Dublin and the memorial service for German soldiers of two world wars at Glencree in County Wicklow.[198] During the 1960s the name of Wolfe Tone was invoked in a number of other ways such, as the founding of the folk group, the Wolfe Tones, whose repertoire consisted largely of 'rebel songs', and the setting up of a number of radical political debating societies in Northern Ireland, called Wolfe Tone clubs.

Throughout the 1950s and the 1960s a number of publications appeared on the 1798 rebellion. Charles Dickson produced in 1955 *The Wexford rising in 1798* and in 1960 *Revolt in the north: Antrim and Down in 1798*. These accounts, which contained not only Dickson's narrative but also valuable reprints of historical documents, set the rebellion in the context of Irish history going back to the Anglo-Normans.[199] In the late 1950s a lecture delivered by a republican prisoner at the Curragh Camp, Seosamh O Cuinneagain, was printed in pamphlet form.[200] The author used the example of Tone to comment on a wide range of matters in contemporary Ireland including the Irish language and the Irish government's financial and foreign policies. An unusual insight into the period of the United Irishmen appeared in 1960 with publication of Mary McNeill's biography of Mary Ann McCracken, sister of United Irishman Henry Joy McCracken.[201] In his major full scale account of the 1798, *The year of liberty*, published in 1969, Thomas Pakenham saw the rebellion as a 'ferocious civil war'.[202] In 1972 a selection of Tone's writings appeared under the editorship of Prionsias Mac Aonghusa and Liam O Riagain.[203]

From 1966 onwards press coverage of the Bodenstown ceremonies increased. This reflected a growing popularity of the event, perhaps sparked off as a consequence of the 1916 commemorations in 1966 and then maintained because of the growing crisis in Northern Ireland.[204] These annual events continued for a period to involve the army, a Fianna Fáil party and a republican parade at Bodenstown on the Sunday closest to 20 June, but each event took place at different times during the day. In the early 1970s, however, reflecting the new divisions in republicanism, the two wings of Sinn Féin marked the event separately: Sinn Féin (Gardner Place) continued to parade on the same occasion as the army and Fianna Fáil while Sinn Féin (Kevin Street) paraded on the Sunday before the main commemoration. By the mid 1970s, the army had stopped attending those June commemorations.[205] By 1980 Sinn Féin (Kevin Street), now called Provisional Sinn Féin, also celebrated the ceremony on the Sunday closest to 20 June, along with Fianna Fáil, while Sinn Féin (Gardner Place), now called Official Sinn Féin or Sinn Féin Workers Party, held its parade on the previous Sunday.[206] In 1981, on the morning of the Tone commemoration on 21 June, the Fianna Fáil party cancelled its appearance at Bodenstown, leaving Provisional Sinn Féin as the only group at the main June event.[207] This Fianna Fáil cancellation was probably in part the result of concern about the Provisional Sinn Féin parade that year, which included a number of prisoners who had escaped from the Crumlin Road jail in Belfast. Fianna Fáil now switched its annual commemoration to a Sunday in September and from this time on has continued to mark the Bodenstown event around this time of year while Provisional Sinn Féin has continued to hold its commemoration on or near 20 June.

Speeches at Bodenstown from 1966 onwards reveal striking differences in approach to Tone and his contemporary relevance. In 1966, at the republican parade, Sean Keenan of Derry made a rare reference to Tone's hope that the name of Irishman would replace the denominations of catholic, protestant and dissenter, but the main speech by Seamus Costello concentrated on attacking on the economic policies of the southern government.[208] In 1968 Sean Garland declared that a socialist republic must be the objective of republicanism.[209] By 1970 violence had erupted in Northern Ireland and from that time on northern matters tended to dominate speeches. The split of the republican movement into two wings led to each side attacking the other as well as the British and Irish governments in their Bodenstown speeches. After 1974 speakers from Official Sinn Féin rejected violence and often cited Tone as their reason for doing so.[210] Provisional Sinn Féin orations continued to support violence and referred to Tone as justification: in 1976 the speaker rejected suggestions that the republican movement was blaspheming the name of Tone, saying that Tone too, 'was a man of violence.'[211] During the late 1980s speeches on behalf of Provisional Sinn Féin continued to justify armed struggle but also backed political action, while from the early 1990s spokespersons began to mention the importance of political negotiations with other involved parties.[212]

During these years subjects covered at the Fianna Fáil commemoration at Bodenstown underwent considerable change. In 1966 no speech was mentioned in the press coverage of the Fianna Fáil wreath laying ceremony. Ruairí Brugha T.D. in 1968 described Tone as the founder of the modern Irish independence movement and a believer in the 'ultimate unity of the nation as a natural right,' and expressed the hope that our 'fellow countrymen, freed from the shackles of the past,… will realize that they are Irish and that they too have a duty to their country'.[213] By 1972, however, Senator Neville Keery declared: 'Respect for Tone, his achievements and virtues is one thing. Realities of changing times is another. No one familiar with the detailed narratives of 1798 would have history repeat itself.'[214] Speeches at these Fianna Fáil commemorations seem to have ceased between 1975 and 1981. They recommenced in September. 1982 with a speech by the taoiseach Charles Haughey. He condemned violence. He also talked 'of the failure to make Northern Ireland work as an entity' and expressed the hope that the descendants of the Belfast republicans of 1798 would eventually 'rejoin their fellow Irishmen.'[215]

Besides the commemorations at Bodenstown during these decades, interest in 1798 was expressed in other ways. Loyalist paramilitaries damaged Tone's grave in 1969 and two years later were responsible for the blowing up of the Tone statue on St Stephen's Green. In 1971 loyalists also destroyed James Hope's gravestone at Mallusk in Co. Antrim. In 1973 the launch of *Freedom the Wolfe Tone way* at a function in Dublin was attended by the heads of both branches of Sinn Féin.[216] New approaches to 1798, however, began slowly to emerge. Sam Hanna Bell's novel *A man flourishing*, set among a northern family during the 1798, was published in 1974. In 1984 Stewart Parker's play *Northern Star* was performed in Belfast for the first time. Concerned with a number of key figures among the supporters of the United Irish cause in the north, in particular Henry Joy McCracken, Parker sought to link protestants to this radical part of their history and to challenge simplistic ideas of continual protestant-catholic conflict, while acknowledging the powerful influence of sectarianism in the past and the present.[217] A number of important historical works were published during the 1980s, particularly by Tom Dunne, Louis Cullen and Marianne Elliott.[218] Responsible for a 1982 study of French links to the United Irishmen, Marianne Elliott was also the author of *Wolfe Tone: prophet of Irish independence*, the first major scholarly biography of Tone, published in 1989. She argued that Tone was 'far less dogmatic about England or the resort to arms than is commonly supposed. His central message was not that Ireland's abiding evil was England, but rather that her people were disunited. Resolve the one and the other would resolve itself naturally.'[219]

During the 1990s interest in the United Irishmen continued to grow. The bicentenary of the founding of the United Irishmen in 1991 was celebrated in Dublin and Belfast by a series of events, conferences and associated published work.[220] Books on 1798 during these years included A.T.Q. Stewart's 1993 *A deeper silence* which looked at the origins of the United Irishmen in Ulster and his 1995 *Summer soldiers* which presented a continuous narrative of the 1798 rising in Down and Antrim.[221] Kevin Whelan's book, *The tree of liberty*, explored the origins of the United Irishmen, especially in Wexford, and also looked at how the '98 was commemorated in the nineteenth century.[222] The bicentenary year 1998 witnessed the appearance of many publications on the subject of the 1798 rebellion.[223] Some of these works dealt with special aspects such as the role of women in the rebellion, the influence of international factors during the late 1790s in Ireland and events in particular areas or counties. The majority of works dealt with the United Irishmen, but some did deal with their opponents, such as Allan Blackstock's study of the yeomanry.[224] The cause and the course of the rebellion in County Wexford were the subject of much writing and considerable debate. Some historians sought to downplay sectarianism and agrarian grievance and to emphasise the importance of popular politicisation and leadership. Others, however such as Tom Dunne, pointed to the influence of sectarian violence and religious bigotry and warned of the dangers of romanticizing 1798.[225] The diaries of Wolfe Tone finally appeared in an unexpurgated volume under the editorship of Tom Bartlett.[226] After decades of research, volume one of the complete writings of Wolfe Tone, edited by Christopher Woods, R.B. McDowell and T.W. Moody, was published during the year.[227] W.A. Maguire was the editor of a major illustrated book on the rebellion based on the material used in an extensive exhibition on 1798 in the Ulster Museum.[228]

Preparations for the celebration of the bicentenary of 1798 began well before 1998. In County Wexford Comoradh '98 was established by Wexford County Council as early as 1989 to co-ordinate commemorative events throughout the county. By the mid 1990s responsibility for co-ordinating commemorative events in the rest of the republic had been undertaken by a government inter-departmental committee under the control of the department of the taoiseach, which also looked after commemorations for the Great Famine. In 1995 the Belfast City Council set up a multi-party committee to plan commemorations of the 1798 rebellion. Fred Cobain, leader of the council's Ulster unionists, declared his support for this move on the grounds that the United Irishmen were part of a radical tradition in which protestants had played a leading role, but which members of that group had ignored. He believed that the ceasefire made it easier for unionist people to focus now on these historical issues.[229] In 1996 the United Irish Commemorative Society, a non-political body of several hundred members, was established in Belfast to organize events leading up to and during 1998. The society received financial support, as did a number of other '98 organisations, from the government sponsored Community Relations Council through its cultural diversity programme.[230]

During 1998 there were extensive celebrations of the bicentenary of the 1798 rebellion. Commemorative events were held in Ireland and also in many parts of the world, including Australia, the U.S.A. and France. In September 1998 President Mary McAleese unveiled what was described as the world's largest 1798 monument in Sydney, Australia.[231] In the Irish republic the government's commemoration committee played an important role in co-ordinating, organising and financing events. The committee declared that its aim was to emphasise the democracy and pluralism of the United Irishmen, the international dimension of the rebellion and the Ulster dimension of 1798.[232] Commemoration of 1798 was marked extensively by local groups. This was especially so in County Wexford, where, as one commentator remarked, 'during the summer of 1998 every parish and half parish in County Wexford had a programme of events to mark the bicentenary of

1798.'[233] To commemorate the 1798 rebellion, a £3 million high
tech visitors centre was opened at Enniscorthy, County Wexford.
Inter-church services were held to remember all who had died.
Tone's call to substitute the name of Irishman in place of the different denominations was often repeated. In sharp contrast to 1948
and 1898 few politicians were involved directly in these commemorations throughout the country. At the Bodenstown commemorations in 1998 the taoiseach Bertie Ahern used the opportunity to
extol the virtues of the Belfast Agreement. He stated his belief that
Wolfe Tone and the United Irishmen were convinced of the bright
future that lay before the Irish people 'if a bad system of government and sectarian dissension could be got rid of, and reform, liberty and equality introduced': he believed that such a future was
now in prospect.[234] In his Bodenstown oration Gerry Adams
referred to Tone as the founder of the republican movement, who
linked 'protestant and dissenter with catholics under the United
Irish banner' and then concentrated on the rights of the Garvaghey
Road residents in relation to Orange marches. [235]

   In Northern Ireland 1998 also saw considerable commemoration
for the 1798 rebellion, although probably not on the same scale as
in the south.[236] Ecumenical services, educational tours, dramas and
lectures in relation to 1798 occurred during the year. The
Community Relations Council sponsored various events and publications. Belfast City Council gave substantial financial support for
a major '98 exhibition, held in the Ulster Museum. Other local
councils, both unionist and nationalist controlled, also backed
events and exhibitions. The United Irish Commemorative Society
ran a series of lectures and displays, as did the Linen Hall Library.
In Ballynahinch, County Down, a town committee organised a
series of wall murals to commemorate the battle in the town, two
hundred years previously. Another such community effort was the
erection for the first time of a headstone at the grave of United
Irishman William Orr in Old Templepatrick Churchyard by
members of the non-subscribing Templepatrick presbyterian
congregation. In west Belfast some wall murals about the United
Irishmen were also painted. The education committee of the

Orange Order marked the '98 bicentenary with publications and events, recalling the actions of ancestors who had been government supporters as well as those who had been United Irishmen. Sinn Féin commemorated the bicentenary with a number of events and the erection of some memorials. One of the few incidents of controversy arose over the construction of a republican monument in County Fermanagh which included not only the names of three United Irishmen, but also the names of three members of the I.R.A., the first killed in the 1950s and the other two during the recent troubles.[237]

V

Over this period of two hundred years public perceptions of the 1798 rebellion have altered greatly. Nowhere is this more obvious than in the case of the changing popularity of Wolfe Tone. He is regarded by many today as one of the most famous figures in Irish history. As we have seen, however, interest in Tone, as expressed in annual pilgrimages to his grave and political references to him, was limited until the end of the nineteenth century. It is really only from around 1910, thanks to the efforts of a number of radical republicans, in particular Patrick Pearse, that he becomes important. The attendance of many of the new political Irish leaders at the annual Bodenstown commemorative events, post 1922, reflects the signifance which people now placed in the example and writings of Tone. His views on physical force, independence and nationality fitted well the needs of this revolutionary generation. Divisions among the group were shown in their different interpretations of Tone. For most of them, however, Tone's idea of breaking the link with England was much more attractive than his idea of uniting catholic, protestant and dissenter. It is this latter idea, however, which makes Tone popular for many people today. Some see him as a modern type of republican free from sectarian overtones, while others regard him as the symbol of a concept of Irishness which accommodates all denominations.

Commemoration of the 1798 rebellion was clearly very different in 1998 from previous anniversaries. The taoiseach Bertie Ahern drew attention to these differences in a speech in late November 1998:

> 1798 cannot be claimed by any single tradition in Ireland. The catholic nationalist version which dominated the centenary, the 1938 and the 1948 commemorations created the 1798 which people think they know. By getting behind these commemorations, we reopen 1798 as an event in the history of presbyterians as much as much as in the history of the catholics. By elevating politics out of the sectarian rut in which it has been largely confined since 1798, the dead weight of the continuous past can be lifted and the political buoyancy restored.[238]

The 1998 commemoration of 1798 revealed a sense of shared history which had not been seen before. Previous anniversaries had been marked on the one side by a strident nationalism which sought to monopolise the event and on the other by a strident unionism which sought to ignore what had happened. Now people from the protestant and unionist communities were willing to acknowledge the part played by their ancestors in the rebellion while people from the catholic and nationalist/republican communities were willing to recognize the former's role. There was a widespread concern to understand both sides, to remember all who had died and to acknowledge faults and harm done to others. During these celebrations there was much less direct political involvement than beforeand the commemorations did not cause the deep divisions and conflict seen on earlier occasions. To some extent this occurred because in the previous two decades before 1998 and during the bicentenary year there was an effort among a number of individuals, including writers, academics and interested members of the public, to rescue 1798 from the restricted and sectional interpretation into which it had fallen. It was also in part a result of the peace process and many, among both party and government circles and the population at large, saw the benefits of making these commemorations inclusive and non-threatening.

This new approach to the commemoration of the 1798 rebellion and the United Irishmen must be seen as part of a growing trend in

Ireland, north and south, to move from simplistic, exclusive views of the past. In the last decade other important historical events have been commemorated in more thoughtful and inclusive ways which have helped to break down some of the hostility which previous narrow and sectional attitudes have engendered. Two examples of this are the one hundred and fiftieth anniversary of the Great Famine and the fiftieth anniversary of the second world war. An awareness of how people in the past have used these events to bolster political and sectional ends has helped to fuel this change. In other ways also there has been a challenge to many of the accepted perceptions of the past. New history writing has questioned some of the myths surrounding well known episodes. Conferences and exhibitions have cast light on contentious historical subjects and in the schools there is a new appreciation of Irish history. All these changes have been important for how people marked the bicentenary of the 1798 rebellion.

3

PUBLIC HOLIDAYS, COMMEMORATION
AND IDENTITY IN IRELAND, NORTH AND SOUTH
1920–60

Public holidays and commemorations of important anniversaries often reflect the values, secular or religious, of a society. Christmas Day and Easter Monday, for example, have special Christian significance in many countries of the world. May Day is also reserved as a holiday in honour of workers in a number of countries. Some public holidays, however, are specific to particular countries, such as Bastille Day on 14 July in France and Independence Day on 4 July in the United States of America, and often refer to events of significance in the history of these countries. Indeed, most countries mark by way of annual commemoration the anniversaries of important episodes, events or people in their history. On Remembrance Day in Great Britain, for instance, people recall all those British and allied servicemen who died in the two world wars. Whether celebrating the early or recent history of a society, these occasions often help to engender a sense of common purpose and identity, even though there may be differences of opinion about the exact significance of the events being celebrated. In Ireland, however, while Christmas Day and Easter Monday have been celebrated by the vast bulk of the population, this has not been the case with some of the other principal public holidays and acts of annual commemoration.

This chapter looks at how four public holidays or annual

commemorative events have been marked in some form or other in both political states in Ireland during the period, 1920–60. The special dates on which these subjects are recalled are as follows: 17 March, when St Patrick, Ireland's patron saint, is commemorated; Easter Sunday, when the Easter Rising in Dublin in 1916 is commemorated; 12 July, when the Battle of the Boyne is celebrated; 11 November, or a Sunday nearest to that date, when people remember those who died in two world wars. Two of these dates mark historical episodes or personalities of antiquity, while the other two commemorate more historical events. We will explore what these commemorations tell us about people's identity and sense of history over this period. Particular attention will be paid to the way in which the respective governments viewed the four commemorations, to the way in which the commemorations were claimed by various groups and to how dominant groups within each state viewed minority groups and opinions. The period dealt with covers the four decades from the creation of Northern Ireland and the Irish State, later the Irish Republic, in the early 1920s until 1960.

I

In the new Northern Ireland of the early 1920s the twelfth of July celebrations to mark the anniversary of the Battle of the Boyne were already an important annual event. Since the 1880s the Orange Order had enjoyed widespread support and these July parades were well attended. The particular importance, however, of this date in the calendar of the new state had not yet been established in the early 1920s. There is evidence that Sir James Craig and the government sought to place some distance between themselves and the Orange movement. In July 1922 Craig was asked in the Northern Ireland parliament to use his influence to have 12 July made a general holiday. He rejected this call and stated: 'In view of the large number of existing statutory holidays, and the fact that the 12th of July has for many years been observed as such, there does not appear to be any necessity to take the action suggested.' Three years later when the matter was raised again in parliament, the minister of home affairs, R.D. Bates, agreed that the date should become a special holiday.[1] In October 1924 the cabinet had decided that there was no objection to the proposal but any such measure was postponed until the following year. In August 1925 the cabinet discussed whether the Westminster parliament should be asked to make 12 July a permanent bank holiday or whether this should be done annually by proclamation, and decided to opt for the latter course of action.[2] By the late 1920s 12 July had become a statutory as well as a general holiday.

There is other evidence that Craig and his fellow ministers tried to downplay links between themselves and the Orange Order in this early period. Craig and most of his cabinet were Orangemen but at this time they took a minor role in these annual July proceedings. On 12 July 1922 Craig spoke at the Belfast demonstrations and described enthusiastically how he and his wife had attended the July celebrations every year since their marriage.[3] In the following year, there was no report of Craig attending the July celebrations and few other ministers spoke from Orange platforms. In July 1923, however, Craig issued a message intended especially for Orange 'brethren' in the U.S.A. and Canada, but which was also read at local parades: 'It is our earnest desire to live in peace and amity with the Free State, and to encourage in every way a better understanding between all classes and creeds.'[4] In 1924 there was again no report of Craig's appearance at the twelfth of July celebrations. In 1925 he sent apologies from England for his non-attendance and explained his absence as due to the recent death of his brother, although, in fact, his brother had died nearly two weeks before the 12 July anniversary.[5] In 1926 the press noted Craig's apologies for his non-attendance but gave no explanation.[6] During these years few of his prominent colleagues spoke on 12 July platforms. Finally, however, in 1927 Craig made a major speech on 12 July at the demonstration in Belfast and from this time on he and other leading ministers attended and spoke regularly on these occasions.[7]

This picture of limited involvement by the unionist leadership

in twelfth of July proceedings in the early 1920s fits in with other
proof that the government was trying to avoid becoming complete-
ly identified with only the protestant section of the population.
Among examples of this are the attempt by Lord Londonderry to
establish non-denominational school education and the appointment of catholic Sir Denis Henry, formerly unionist M.P. for
Londonderry South, to the post of lord chief justice of Northern
Ireland.[8] These gestures of moderation, however, did not continue,
partly because of a lack of nationalist and catholic co-operation and
partly because of ultra protestant opposition and concern about
unionist unity in the face of political threats from labour and other
groups. When Craig returned to an Orange platform in 1927 it was
to take the opportunity to warn against the danger of division in
unionist ranks and to justify the government's plan to abolish pro-
portional representation in elections to the Northern Ireland parliament: it is generally accepted that this move was not designed as
an attack on nationalists but was an attempt to curtail unionist
splinter groups.[9] From 1927 onwards members of the government
used these twelfth of July parades to espouse their political stance
and promote unionist unity. By the early 1930s Craig made a point
of attending the twelfth of July proceedings every year in a different county of Northern Ireland. Clearly the government was avail-
ing of these occasions to their advantage, but matters were not
always under their control. Because of the fear of sectarian violence
the authorities tried to stop the twelfth of July demonstrations in
Belfast in 1935 but had to back down due to strong Orange opposition. The celebrations that year were in fact followed by nine days
of serious rioting in Belfast.[10]

At the July parades during the 1930s, speeches by politicians,
clergymen and members ranged over various religious and political
subjects. Loyalty to the crown and empire was reaffirmed regularly.
In 1933 Craig declared: 'British we are and British we remain.'[11]
Protestant principles were upheld and catholicism was denounced.
In 1932 Craig stated: 'Ours is a protestant government and I am an
Orangeman.'[12] Political affairs in the south were often mentioned
and the fate of southern protestants was frequently referred to.

Links with the empire were stressed. In 1939 Craig declared that: 'the British empire, and all it stands for, is the sun and air of our existence'.[13] The importance of the twelfth of July commemorations and the Orange Order for unionists was stressed in a report in the *Northern Whig on* 13 July 1933:

> Throughout people recognised the need for keeping at full pitch the unity and strength of the Order. It has proved in the past the nucleus around which unionism of the province gathered when danger of submission in a nationalist and Roman Catholic dominated Ireland threatened.

The outbreak of war resulted in the curtailment of parades, 1940–2. These restrictions, voluntary in 1940 and mandatory in 1941 and 1942, covered not only the main twelfth of July processions but also parades before 12 July, including the annual march to a church service at Drumcree, County Armagh, on the Sunday before 12 July.[14] Thereafter the annual twelfth of July parades resumed, although in a limited form, for the rest of the war.

During the 1940s and 1950s the government and the unionist party remained strongly identified with the twelfth of July proceedings and the Orange movement. Speeches by Lord Brookeborough during the 1950s referred to I.R.A. attacks and also the greater economic benefits which the north enjoyed compared to the south.[15] Not until the late 1950s and early 1960s did questions begin to emerge from both Orange and unionist circles to challenge the link between the two organisations. On 13 July 1960 an editorial in the *Belfast News Letter* referred to the new thinking on these matters and put it down to a more stable political climate in Northern Ireland and better north/south relations. In Brookeborough's last years as a premier some Orange leaders urged that the religious aspects of the twelfth should be increased at the expense of the political and by the early 1960s fewer prominent politicians were involved in the twelfth of 12 July proceedings.[16] At the same time some politicians urged that unionism should not be restricted to protestants. In July 1960 R. S. Dixon, M. P., declared that 'civil and religious liberty must be for all sections of the community', while in July 1961 W.M. May, M.P., stated that 'we must do our best to impress on our Roman Catholic citizens that this order stands for toleration'.[17] Historical ghosts resonated at the Orange demonstration at Bangor, County Down, in 1960! A report in the press recounted:

> One of the most unexpected people to turn up at the Bangor demonstration was Michael Collins. When his name was announced over the loudspeakers there was consternation on the faces of the platform party and gathering. But smiles were soon in evidence when it was explained that Michael was a little boy who had got lost.[18]

The first Armistice Day on 11 November 1919, commemorated the end of the first world war, and was widely marked in many parts of Northern Ireland by both nationalists and unionists. Services were held in churches of all denominations. The *Irish Times* described the situation in Belfast on 11 Nov. 1919:

> The Armistice silence was observed in an impressive manner in Belfast. All the tramcars were stopped, and in the large industrial concerns, such as the shipyards and the spinning factories, the workers stopped for two minutes and stood by their machines.'[19]

From the early 1920s the event was commemorated not only with a two-minute silence and church services, but also with parades to new war memorials. There is evidence that in the early days there were efforts to keep these event open to all sections of the community. At the unveiling of the Enniskillen war memorial in 1922, for example, protestant and catholic war orphans laid wreaths.[20] At a ceremony in Ballymena on 11 November 1924, Major General Sir Oliver Nugent who had commanded the 36th (Ulster) Division at the Somme, declared that 'the service given by the Ulstermen in the war was not confined to one creed or one denomination; it was given by Ulstermen of all denominations and all classes'.[21] The ceremony for the unveiling of the Portadown war memorial in 1924 involved the catholic parish priest along with the other clergy, and wreaths were laid by representatives of the Orange Order and the Ancient Order of Hibernians.[22] On 12 November 1924 the *Irish*

News, reported commemorations in both Northern Ireland and the Irish Free State with the headline 'Brotherhood of bereavement – north and south pause to salute the dead'.

In spite of these comments and inclusive incidents, however, the Armistice Day commemorations became largely linked with unionism. To some extent this arose because of a reluctance in certain catholic and nationalist quarters to acknowledge the catholic role in the war. For example, Cardinal Patrick O'Donnell, catholic archbishop of Armagh, refused to attend the unveiling of the County Armagh war memorial in 1926.[23] More importantly, many unionists came to see Armistice Day as an occasion for the affirmation of their own sense of Ulster or British identity. As Professor Keith Jeffery has commented: 'For them the blood sacrifice of the Somme was equal and opposite to that of Easter 1916.'[24] At the unveiling of Coleraine war memorial in 1922 Sir James Craig declared that 'those who passed away have left behind a great message to all of them to stand firm, and to give away none of Ulster's soil.'[25] Only protestant clergy attended the unveiling of the cenotaph at the Belfast City Hall in 1929 and there were no official representatives from the 16th (Irish) Division in which Belfast catholics had tended to serve.[26]

The government played no direct role in organising events on Armistice Day and speeches were rarely made on the occasion but the large parades and well-attended services on the day with army and police involved were seen by many not only as an expression of grief but also as a mark of the British link among the unionist community. It would be wrong, however, to write off entirely catholic and nationalist involvement in the Armistice Day commemorations. Catholic ex-servicemen continued to mark the occasion in some places. In Newry in the 1930s on Armistice Day ex-servicemen held a parade before making their way to their respective catholic and protestant churches for memorial services.[27] During the 1930s Armistice Day wreaths were laid in Belfast for the men for the 16th (Irish) division and in Derry for the 'Irish catholic officers and men who fell in the great war', while at Portadown a wreath was laid for the Connaught Rangers, in which Portadown catholics had served.[28]

After the second world war, Armistice Day was replaced by Remembrance Day and held on the Sunday closest to 11 November. Names of those who had served or died in the war were added to existing memorials. Parades and services continued as they had done on Armistice Day, and they remained largely the concern of the protestant and unionist community. While the government had no formal involvement in these events it was quite common for the prime minister or a cabinet minister to take the salute of ex-servicemen on these occasions. There is little evidence of involvement of catholic clergy in public ceremonies at cenotaphs or at council services. At the same time we should note that in some places, such as Dungannon, Newry and Sion Mills, parades of catholic and protestant ex-servicemen continued to take place as they had done in the 1930s.[29] The degree of polarisation between the two communities over this commemoration is revealed starkly in a comparison of coverage of these events in Belfast nationalist and unionist papers in the mid 1950s. In 1955 and 1956 the unionist papers, the *Belfast News Letter* and the *Northern Whig* gave extensive coverage to Remembrance Day in various places in Northern Ireland as well as in London, while the nationalist paper, the *Irish News*, ignored the occasion and carried not a single report on any event connected with the commemoration.[30]

By the early 1900s St Patrick's Day on 17 March was widely celebrated throughout Ireland, north and south. In 1903 an act of the Westminster parliament made St Patrick's Day a bank holiday, a measure supported by unionist and nationalist M.P.s. After 1921 St Patrick's Day was still observed in Northern Ireland but on a lower key than in the south where it took on special importance. During the 1920s and 1930s in Northern Ireland the shamrock continued to be worn widely and the day remained a bank holiday when banks, government and municipal offices and schools were closed, although most shops and factories seem to have been unaffected.[31] In catholic churches St Patrick's Day was an important feast day which was well-attended. The Ancient Order of Hibernians continued to organise demonstrations on this date and nationalist politicians often used the occasion to make speeches. From 1925 the B.B.C. in Northern Ireland commenced an annual series of special St Patrick's days broadcasts.[32]

The Patrician Year of 1932, which marked the anniversary of St Patrick's arrival in Ireland was marked by all the churches. At Saul, the site of St Patrick's first church, the Church of Ireland built a new church while the catholic church erected a statue of St Patrick on a nearby hill top. Each of the main denominations took advantage of the occasion to reaffirm its belief that St Patrick belonged exclusively to its tradition.[33] Sporting activities on St Patrick's day, including the Ulster schools rugby cup, and special theatrical events, dances and dinners were well attended in the 1920s and 1930s. On 18 March 1939 the *Belfast News Letter* reported that 'in Belfast and all over the province Ulster folk said goodbye to St Patrick's Day with dances and other entertainments'. Special ceremonies of the trooping of the colour and presentation of the shamrock to Irish regiments remained a tradition (begun by Queen Victoria at the end of her reign).There was, however, no official involvement in or recognition of St Patrick's Day, apart from a number of dinners or dances on the day, organised by the Duke of Abercorn, as governor of Northern Ireland.[34] On the unionist and government side there was no attempt to hold parades or make speeches on 17 March. The speeches of southern politicians on the day denouncing partition or declaring Ireland's attachment to Rome were reported regularly in the northern press and sometimes criticised in editorials but there was no attempt by the government in this period to respond.

After the war, banks and government offices continued to close on St Patrick's Day, while the wearing of the shamrock remained popular and the tradition of presenting it to the Irish regiments abroad continued. Catholic churches still observed it as a special feast day and the Ancient Order of Hibernians organised parades and demonstrations as before. In the late 1940s and early 1950s the Northern Ireland premier, Lord Brookeborough, used the occasion of St Patrick's Day to issue public addresses to Ulster people abroad, while members of his cabinet spoke at dinners organised by Ulster associations in Great Britain.[35] By the mid 1950s, however, these attempts to match the political use made of St Patrick's Day by the southern government had mostly ceased. In the late 1950s a government information officer urged the cabinet that it might be wise to 'quietly forget' St Patrick's Day and abolish it as a bank holiday.[36] The suggestion was rejected, but it is clear from newspaper reports in the 1950s that for many people St Patrick's Day was 'business as usual'. Many schools dropped it as a holiday and shops and businesses remained open.[37] Correspondents in the unionist press denounced the political overtones of the day in the south and elsewhere. One letter on 17 March 1961 stated that 'the day is now chiefly memorable to the average Ulsterman as the day on which repeated threats against his stand for constitutional liberty are pronounced in the republic and on which Ulster's position is vilified throughout the English speaking world'.[38]

Nonetheless, it should be noted that there were some in unionist and protestant church circles who believed that more attention should be given to the event. From the mid-1950s the editorial in the *Belfast Telegraph* often urged that the day should be a full public holiday, a request backed by the Church of Ireland diocesan synod of Down and Dromore.[39] In 1961 a resolution of the Young Unionists' Conference deplored the apathy in Northern Ireland towards St Patrick's Day.[40] In the 1950s the Church of Ireland inaugurated an annual St Patrick's Day pilgrimage and special service at Downpatrick and Saul, which was well-attended. Such events were still strongly limited by denominational barriers although small elements of change were occurring. In 1956 the nationalist members of Downpatrick council refused an invitation to participate in a joint-wreath laying ceremony at St Patrick's grave on the grounds that the catholic church 'had arranged adequate celebrations for the Feast and they could not add anything to them'. Eight years later, however, when the Archbishop of Canterbury was the special guest at the St Patrick's Day service at the Church of Ireland cathedral in Downpatrick, nationalist councillors turned up to greet the archbishop at the entrance to the cathedral, although they felt unable to enter the building.[41]

Commemoration at Eastertime of the 1916 rising was low-key and without much public notice in Northern Ireland until 1928 when well-publicised ceremonies were held at republican plots in Milltown cemetery in Belfast and in the city cemetery in Derry. In the following year and throughout the 1930s, the government, using the Special Powers Act, prohibited these commemorations. In support of the ban the minister of home affairs, R.D. Bates, stated that those involved were 'celebrating one of the most treacherous and bloody rebellions that ever took place in the history of the world' and claimed that there was I.R.A. involvement in the commemorations.[42] The nationalist leader, Joe Devlin, challenged this view in parliament in 1932 and argued that that the ban on the commemorations was a denial of people's right to free speech and referred to one such event in Newry as simply 'an annual commemoration for all those who died for Ireland'.[43]

Every Easter during the 1930s commemorative meetings were announced and then declared illegal by the government, but there were often attempts to get round the ban.[44] In 1935, for example, about five hundred people gathered on Easter Monday some fifty yards beyond the cemetery gates at Milltown graveyard where they recited a decade of the rosary, while in Derry republicans held their commemorations a week before Easter to get round the ban at Eastertime.[45] On a number of occasions in Derry and Armagh wreath-laying ceremonies were performed on Saturday night, hours before the ban came into operation on Easter Sunday.[46] Tension arose frequently over the flying of the tricolour and the wearing of the Easter lily. The most serious confrontation between the police and republican organisers came in 1942, when active I.R.A. units became involved in the commemorations, leading to shooting in both Dungannon and Belfast, and the murder of a catholic police constable in Belfast.[47]

By 1948 the government had decided not to impose a general ban on Easter commemorations of 1916. From this time on commemorative events were held in a number of centres by a range of organisations. In 1950, for example, the main event at Milltown cemetery in Belfast was organised by the National Graves Association.[48]

This was followed by a separate service organised under the auspices of the republican socialist party, addressed by Harry Diamond M.P. who referred to 'the shadow of a foreign occupation of a portion of their country'. Finally there was another ceremony held by the 'Old Pre-Truce IRA'. In Newry a commemorative service was followed by a large parade, led by members of Newry urban council, and including members of the catholic boy scouts, the Foresters and the Hibernians. There were also Easter commemorative events in County Armagh and County Tyrone and Derry city. Similar events occurred during the 1950s with few problems, although sometimes there was conflict between organisers and police over the flying of the tricolour, as for example in Lurgan in 1952 and 1953 when the Royal Ulster Constabulary confiscated flags and made arrests. In Newry in 1957 arrests were also made over the flying of the tricolour at the Easter commemorations, and in the following year a parade to commemorate 1916 was prohibited in the town, although the ban was ignored.[49]

II

In the new Irish Free State St Patrick's Day quickly took on special significance. By 1922 it had been made a general holiday and from 1925, thanks to the Free State licensing act, all public houses were closed on that day. In Dublin, an annual army parade now replaced the processions organised by the lord lieutenant and lord mayor. Throughout the country there were parades, often involving army marches to church for mass. Dances, sporting activities, theatrical events and excursions were run on the day. The Irish language was specially promoted on the day, frequently with events organised by the Gaelic League. In 1926 the southern premier W.T. Cosgrave made the first official radio broadcast on St Patrick's Day. He called for mutual understanding and harmony and declared that:

The destinies of the country, north and south, are now in the hands of Irishmen, and the responsibility for success or failure will rest with ourselves. If we are to succeed there must be a brotherly toleration of each other's ideas as to how our ambition may be realised, and a brotherly co-operation in every effort towards its realisation.[50]

In his St Patrick's Day's speech, 1930, Cosgrave declared that 'as we have been Irish and Roman, so it will remain', but he took care to preface his statement with the remarks that he was speaking for the majority of people in the state.[51] In 1931 in a St Patrick's Day broadcast to the Irish in America, and reported in the Irish press, Cosgrave again sought to make a reconciliatory gesture 'whatever be your creed in religion or politics, you are of the same blood – the healing process must go on'.[52]

With the accession to power of Eamon de Valera and Fianna Fáil in 1932 St Patrick's Day took on added significance. Links between church and state were publicly stressed with the annual procession on St Patrick's Day of de Valera and his executive council, complete with a cavalry troop, to the Dublin pro-cathedral for mass.[53] The Patrician Year of 1932, which included the Eucharistic Congress, gave an opportunity for large demonstrations, with considerable official involvement, emphasising connections between Ireland and Rome.[54] This religious aspect was taken up again by de Valera in his St Patrick's Day broadcast of 1935 in which he reminded people that Ireland had been a Christian and catholic nation since St Patrick's time: 'She remains a catholic nation,' he declared.[55] De Valera now used the St Patrick's Day broadcasts, which were transmitted to the U.S.A. and Australia, to launch vigorous attacks on the British government and partition. These speeches reached a peak in 1939, when in Rome for St Patrick's Day de Valera declared how he had made a pledge beside the grave of Hugh O'Neill that he would never rest until 'that land which the Almighty so clearly designed as one shall belong undivided to the Irish people'. He urged his listeners to do likewise.[56] At the same time, however, the links between catholicism and Irish identity as expressed on St Patrick's Day was not absolute. For example, the protestant president of Ireland, Douglas Hyde, attended a St Patrick's Day service in the Church Of Ireland cathedral of St Patrick's in Dublin in 1939.[57]

During the war celebrations on St Patrick's Day were low-key although de Valera continued to make his annual broadcast. In 1943 he spoke of the restoration of the national territory and the national language as the greatest of the state's uncompleted tasks. He also talked of his dream of a land 'whose fields and villages would be joyous with the sounds of industry, the romping of sturdy children, the contests of athletic youths and the laughter of comely maidens'.[58] After the war St Patrick's Day became a major national holiday once again. In 1950 the military parade in Dublin was replaced by a trade and industries parade. In their St Patrick's Day speeches in the1950s, heads of government, Eamon de Valera and J.A. Costello, continued to use the event to make strong denunciations of partition. In his St Patrick's Day broadcast in 1950 Costello declared that 'our country is divided by foreign interference'.[59]

By the 1950s, government ministers and spokesmen, such as Sean MacEntee, were also making public speeches on the day at a range of venues in Britain and the U.S.A., usually concentrating on attacking partition.[60] In 1955 a rare discordant note was struck by Bishop Cornelius Lucy of Cork when in his St Patrick's Day address he suggested that emigration was a greater evil than partition.[61] Irish leaders in their speeches continued to emphasise links between Ireland and Rome; by the mid 1950s it was common for the president or taoiseach to be in Rome on St Patrick's Day. The 1961 Patrician celebrations marked a high point in this religious aspect of the festival. It began with the arrival on 13 March of a papal legate, Cardinal MacIntyre, who in the words of the *Capuchin Annual* was 'welcomed with the protocol reception given only to a head of state.' This included a welcome at the airport from the taoiseach and a full military guard.[62]

Annual commemoration of the Dublin Rising of 1916 proved a very contentious issue in the new Irish state, reflecting some of the political divisions which had emerged over the Anglo-Irish treaty (1921) and also personal concerns about any such event.[63] During commemorations in 1922 a number of prominent politicians from both the pro-treaty and anti-treaty sides addressed large crowds in various places, but the event was not marked publicly the following year, owing to the civil war. On Easter Monday 1924 the government organised a ceremony at Arbour Hill (burial place of the executed rebels) for a specially invited list of guests, including politicians, soldiers and relatives of the deceased.[64] Few relatives of the deceased turned up, however, and in this and following years the event was marred by disputes about who should be invited. Also in 1924 republicans organised a march through Dublin to Glasnevin cemetery for the laying of wreaths on the republican plot. Subsequently, large parades to Glasnevin were organised and attended each Easter by republican groups, including Sinn Féin and (after 1927) Fianna Fáil. The Cumann na nGaedheal government did not participate in these marches, although there was some official remembrance of the Easter Rising in 1926 and after, in the form of broadcasts on the subject on the new Radio Éireann.

When De Valera came to power in 1932, the situation did not change greatly. In Dublin there were two parades, the first organised by the semi-official National Commemoration Committee and attended by de Valera and members of Fianna Fail, which marched to Arbour Hill, and the second run by other republican groups, including the I.R.A., which marched to Glasnevin.[65] The Fianna Fail government changed the guest list to the Arbour Hill ceremony but also ran into difficulties with relatives of the deceased about who should be present.[66] In 1935 there was a large Irish army parade on Easter Sunday to the General Post Office where a statue of Cuchulainn was unveiled and speeches were made by government ministers. This statue, supposedly symbolic of the rising, had in fact been sculpted between 1910 and 1911 and purchased much later for this purpose.[67] The twentieth anniversary of the rising saw some additional measures of commemoration, in particular radio programmes during Easter week on Radio Éireann. The event continued to be commemorated in Dublin principally by the two rival marches to Arbour Hill and Glasnevin. Outside Dublin the Rising was commemorated at Eastertime by competing republican groups. For example, in Cork the Old I.R.A. Men's Association marched each Easter to several monuments and graves of their dead comrades.[68]

On the twenty fifth anniversary of the Easter Rising in 1941, major celebrations were held in Dublin. On Easter Sunday a military parade, described as the largest ever held in Dublin, took place.[69] There were speeches at the G.P.O. from President Douglas Hyde and members of the government. De Valera also made a broadcast from the G.P.O. calling for improvements in the armed forces and for vigilance in preserving Ireland's independence. For the remainder of the war public celebrations were severely limited. After 1945 rival parades recommenced in Dublin, with no special government involvement, apart from the appearance of Fianna Fáil ministers at Arbour Hill. In 1949, no doubt for symbolic reasons, the official inauguration of the Irish Republic occurred at one minute past midnight on Easter Monday. Only from 1954 did a military parade at the GPO in Dublin at Easter first become an annual event. It was part of the An Tóstal celebrations of that year but was continued in following years.[70] The fortieth anniversary of the rising was celebrated extensively in 1956. President Sean T. O'Kelly, the taoiseach, John A. Costello and other government ministers were on the saluting platform at the G.P.O., there were many radio programmes on the Easter Rising and various groups in different parts of the country held parades.[71] After this the com-memorations returned to the practice of a military parade in Dublin and other marches in Dublin and elsewhere organised by various groups.

During the first world war an estimated two hundred thousand people from Ireland, a majority from the twenty counties which became the Irish Free State, served in the British armed forces. On the first Armistice day on 11 November 1919, in line with a papal decree, mass was held at all catholic churches in Ireland to mark the occasion.[72] A two minute silence at eleven o'clock was observed widely. Subsequently, with the war of independence and the setting up of the new Irish Free State, commemoration of this event became very controversial. As Jane Leonard has commented: 'divi-sion rather than dignity surrounded the commemoration of the war in Ireland'.[73] The civil unrest of the early 1920s restricted public expressions of commemoration. From 1923 onwards, however, Armistice Day was marked not just by a two minute silence but also by parades and assemblies of ex-servicemen and their friends and families which were held in Dublin and in other parts of Ireland. Such events were organised by several ex-servicemen's organisations until they were eventually were brought together under the British Legion in 1925. War memorials were erected in many places and the poppy was sold widely.[74]

Official attitudes were ambivalent but generally tolerant in the 1920s. Conscious of nationalist and republican susceptibilities, members of the Free State government looked askance at ideas to build a large war memorial in central Dublin, and insisted that it be erected on the outskirts at Islandbridge.[75] At the same time, conscious of the many Irish people who had died during the war, including members of their own families, the government sent representatives to the wreath-laying ceremonies in Dublin and London. The message on the wreath laid by Colonel Maurice Moore, the Irish government representative, at the temporary cenotaph cross in College Green in Dublin on 11 November read: 'This wreath is placed here by the Free State government to commemorate all the brave men who fell on the field of battle.'[76] In 1923 W.T. Cosgrave and some cabinet colleagues attended an Armistice Day mass in Cork.[77]

Early armistice day commemorations in Dublin met with a certain amount of opposition, expressed in actions such as the snatching of poppies. From the mid 1920s, however, the intensity of this opposition grew, with various republican groups organising anti-Armistice Day rallies to protest against 'the flagrant display of British imperialism disguised as Armistice celebrations' and with physical attacks being made on some of the parades.[78] In 1926 this led to the main ceremony being moved from the centre of Dublin to Phoenix Park. De Valera spoke at one of the anti-Armistice Day rallies in 1930 and the formation of a Fianna Fáil government in 1932 led to a further downgrading of the commemorations. Official representatives were withdrawn from the main wreath laying ceremony in Dublin from November 1932, although the Irish

government continued to be represented at the cenotaph in
London until 1936. Permits for the sale of poppies, previously
allowed for several days in the week before 11 November, were now
reduced to one day only.[79] Those taking part in the annual parade
to Phoenix Park in Dublin were prohibited from carrying union
jacks or British Legion flags which featured a union jack. Work on
the national war memorial park at Islandbridge was completed and
handed over to the government in early 1937, but the official opening was put off a number of times by de Valera, until the outbreak
of the second world war led to its indefinite postponement. The
official opening of the park occurred only in 1988 and without the
direct involvement of the Fianna Fáil government, although at a
later ceremony in 1994, Bertie Ahern, then minister of finance,
declared the work on the memorial to be finished.[80]

Armistice ceremonies were held at Phoenix Park in 1939 and at
Islandbridge in 1940, although without parades.[81] Thereafter public demonstrations in Dublin relating to this event were banned
until after the war. Indeed the government maintained its ban in
November 1945, after the end of the war, because it did not want
to see any public demonstration of Irish involvement in the allied
war effort. In fact, an estimated fifty thousand men and women
went from the twenty counties of Ireland, along with many other
Irish people already living in Great Britain, to serve in British armed
forces during the war.[82] The Irish government, however, continued
to ignore this matter. As elsewhere Armistice day was replaced by
Remembrance Sunday, on the Sunday closest to 11 November, and
the event was marked by a parade of ex-servicemen in Dublin from
Smithfield Market along North Quays to Islandbridge and by dis-
crete wreath-laying ceremonies in other centres.[83] These parades
and other commemorative events continued during the 1950s, but
for many of those involved, as declining numbers attending
Remembrance Day and veterans' memories showed, there was a
clear sense that they had become marginalised and excluded from
the new Irish identity and sense of history that had now become
dominant.[84]

Before 1921 Orange parades had occurred regularly in the three

Ulster counties of Donegal, Cavan and Monaghan, which on to become part of the Irish Free State. These parades were restricted in the early 1920s because of disturbances and violence during the civil war but recommenced in 1923. At the main Orange parade at Clones in County Monaghan in 1923 an Orange spokesman declared that:

> they did not desire to be placed under their present regime, but they paid tribute to whom tribute was due. They were not going to rebel, because it would be useless and would not be right. In face of great difficulties and trials the Free State government had done a great deal, but they had a great deal more to do...[85]

In 1925 it was reckoned that ten thousand people attended an Orange demonstration in July at Newbliss in County Monaghan.[86] At a large twelfth of July demonstration at Rockcorry, County Monaghan, in 1930, resolutions were passed which declared allegiance to King George V as head of the Commonwealth, support for Orange principles, rejoicing in the good relations in County Monaghan and protest against compulsory use of the Irish language.[87] In the 1920s Orange parades were not so common in Donegal, because members from the county, especially the eastern part, often attended twelfth of July parades in Derry or other northern locations. South Donegal Orangemen held July demonstrations at Rossnowlagh and Darney.[88] In spite of incidents at Orange events in Cavan town in 1930 and in Newtowngore in County Leitrim in 1931, twelfth of July Orange demonstrations passed off reasonably peacefully in 1931 in Cootehill, County Cavan, and in Monaghan town.[89] The year 1931, however, proved to be the last time that Orange parades took place in Counties Cavan and Monaghan.

A month after these twelfth of July celebrations in 1931 a large body of republicans, including I.R.A. units, occupied Cootehill on the eve of a planned demonstration on 12 August by members of the Royal Black Institution from counties Cavan and Monaghan.[90] The railway line through the town was blown up and there were reports of armed men on the streets. The authorities reacted

strongly and troops and extra police were dispatched to Cootehill
to restore law and order. Although the Black demonstration did not
take place the government gave assurances to local Orange and
Black leaders that their parades would be protected.[91] In 1932,
however, the Grand County Lodges of Cavan, Donegal and
Monaghan cancelled all demonstrations in their counties. The
minutes of the County Monaghan Grand Lodge show that in June
1932 members received information that 'arms were being distrib-
uted by the same party who had caused all the trouble at Cootehill
with the object of interfering with our July demonstration'.[92] The
Grand Lodge decided to cancel both this demonstration and also all
parades to church services.

   In future years Monaghan lodges did have limited marches to
church services, but, in spite of the fact that members throughout
the 1930s wanted to resume their twelfth of July demonstrations,
this never happened because of fear of the consequences. [93] Orange
activities in counties Cavan and Monaghan were now restricted to
church services and private meetings, and lodges attended the
twelfth of July parades in Northern Ireland. In County Donegal,
however, July Orange parades resumed in the 1930s at
Rossnowlagh in the south of the county. [94]. After the second world
war many of the lodges from Cavan and Monaghan attended the
Rossnowlagh demonstration. By the 1950s the date of this parade
had been moved to the Saturday prior to 12 July, so allowing
Orange members from Northern Ireland to attend the event and
southern members to take part in twelfth of July parades across the
border.

III

The four decades between 1920 and 1960 saw the founding and
consolidation of two new political states in Ireland. While both
Northern Ireland and the Irish Free State, later the Irish Republic,
marked all four of the national holidays or days of commemoration
examined here, the difference in the manner and extent of the celebrations tells us much about how each state and its citizens viewed

their own identity and sense of history. Undoubtedly for many involved, the subject of commemoration or celebration, such as Armistice Day or St Patrick's Day, had a personal and heartfelt meaning. At the same time, these occasions often took on a special significance, and were related to issues of identity and politics as they effected the broader community. Important changes occurred in how such special days were marked. Sometimes these changes were influenced by the leader's attempts to respond to pressures and divisions within their own group, while at other times they were a response by a leader and a group to the actions and statements of their opponents. De Valera's opposition to Armistice Day may have been caused partly by a concern to keep republicans on his side and partly as a reaction to attempts by some in the 1920s to turn 'the 11th November into the 12th July'.[95] Craig's new links with Orangeism and a protestant identity may have been the result partly of a concern to maintain unionist unity and partly as a response to southern politicians who 'boasted of a catholic state'.[96]

Before 1920 St Patrick's Day and Armistice Day enjoyed widespread support. Between 1920 and 1960, however, these occasions were increasingly dominated and endorsed by some sections of the community and rejected by others. St Patrick's Day was used by nationalists/republicans to help boost an exclusive nationalist and catholic view of Irish identity. Partly because of this, and partly because of a concern by some unionists to emphasise British links, many but not all protestants came to disregard St Patrick's Day. Armistice Day was used by unionists to strengthen an exclusive unionist and protestant view of British identity. As a result, and thanks also to an effort by some nationalists to ignore or reject this part of their recent history, many but not all catholics came to ignore Armistice day. In Northern Ireland the anniversary of the battle of the Boyne was institutionalised as an important historical event. In the Irish Free State the anniversary of the Easter Rising was an important historical date, although different groups sought to claim it. In the case of Boyne commemorations in the south and Easter commemorations in the north, both majority communities showed little tolerance for the historical views of their minorities.

During this period of the early years of both states, political relations between north and south and between the different communities were dominated by religious divisions and conflict over constitutional issues. Some of the developments which we have seen here, however, helped to polarise these relations even further. Both St Patrick's Day and Armistice Day had the potential to remind people of a shared history, of common interests and suffering. Instead they were used to emphasise differences and to develop more exclusive versions of identity and history. The twelfth of July and Easter Sunday represented events special to the histories of Northern Ireland and the Irish Free State, respectively, but neither society showed any understanding of the history of the other nor allowed much opportunity for minorities to mark these events. It has been argued that the passion and confrontation aroused by the large number of commemorations in the 1960s, especially in 1966, was one of the factors which helped to destabilise political society in Northern Ireland and led to the outbreak of the troubles.[97] The widely held conflicting views of identity and history, fostered in part by these commemorations of the previous forty years, helped to create the atmosphere of distrust and misunderstanding which made these 1960s commemorations so divisive and harmful for politics.

4

THE BURDEN OF THE PAST:
HISTORY AND POLITICS IN NORTHERN IRELAND

In remarks, speeches and analyses of the conflict in Northern Ireland there are many references to the importance of the past. On the B.B.C. programme, *Newsnight*, 1 July 1998, Jeremy Paxman talked of 'ancestral politics' in Northern Ireland while on B.B.C., *News at nine*, 3 July 1998, Dennis Murray commented on 'divisions that go back to the seventeenth century'. On Ulster Television evening news, on 22 June 1998, John Hume, the leader of the Social Democratic and Labour Party, talked of trying to create a new situation where 'our old quarrels will be gone', and said that people wanted to 'leave the past behind'. On the B.B.C. *Hearts and Minds* current affairs programme, on 1 June 2000, Ian Paisley, leader of the Democratic Unionist Party, referred to unionists' 'traditional enemies'. The report of the international body on decommissioning, which appeared in January 1996, noted, for example, how 'common to many of our meetings were arguments, steeped in history, as to why the other side cannot be trusted. As a consequence, even well-intentioned acts are often viewed with suspicion and hostility'.[1] Such sentiments were endorsed in October of the same year when, Michael Cassidy, the South African church leader, referring to Ireland, remarked that: 'One notices how people are gripped by the past, remembering the past, feeding on the past; people are constantly remembering this betrayal or that battle; this

plantation or that pogrom; this martyr or this murderer'. He concluded that 'these realities of the past feed into the present in
Ireland more than anywhere I have been'.[2]

The perceived relevance of the past for current events in Northern
Ireland was demonstrated in much of the reaction to the Belfast
Agreement of 1998. The *Irish Times* website on the agreement
included an introduction with an historical chronology which
began with the Anglo-Norman invasion of 1169 and concluded on
9 April, on the eve of the acceptance of the agreement by the different parties involved.[3] The *Belfast Telegraph* on 21 May 1998, on
the eve of the referendum on the agreement, talked of a new partnership between the peoples of these islands, British and Irish, 'that
will replace 800 years of enmity with trust and friendship'. It continued: 'We have a chance to break free from the past and to go for
the future'. After the agreement had been accepted Tony Blair
declared: 'I feel the hand of history upon our shoulders. I really
do'.[4] President Clinton has often talked of the 'ancient enmities' in
Northern Ireland. Speaking in Dublin on 4 September 1998 he
argued that Northern Ireland's success in its peace process would
have lessons for other societies dealing with historical problems.
The progress of Northern Ireland's peace process, he believed, was
'helping the world awaken from history's nightmares' by showing
that ancient enmities could be overcome. If it was successfully concluded, he continued: 'we can say to the Middle East, we can say in
the Aegean... "Look at this thing that happened in Northern
Ireland. There were the Troubles for thirty years, conflicts for hundred of years. This can be done".' [5]

This chapter will begin with a look at the history of Northern
Ireland. We will examine how special this history is and assess how
far the current conflict is really rooted in the past. Attention will
focus on the ways in which the different communities in Northern
Ireland have acquired their sense of history, looking at both the
unionist and loyalist side and at the nationalist and republican side.
The consequences of these historical views for conflict between the
communities will be examined. We will also look at the important
changes in people's perceptions of their past which have occurred in

the last decade. This will be followed by a study of the ways in which politicians and political commentators have made reference to the past in recent years. From this we can assess how important history has been and still is for Northern Ireland. Are there, as President Clinton has argued, important lessons here for those attempting to understand and deal with other societies where ancient quarrels are supposed to be important?

I

In common with elsewhere, Northern Ireland today is influenced by its past. We can trace many characteristics of contemporary Northern Ireland to its historical development. This is not to say, however, that current matters here are determined by historical episodes. This is true about other societies. They are influenced but not controlled by their history. In countries such as Germany and Hungary there was bitter religious conflict in the early seventeenth century, but today, in spite of this history, these societies enjoy peaceful internal relations. In English history, for example, the civil war of the mid seventeenth century is acknowledged as an important event, but few politicians refer to this today, as they do to historical events in Northern Ireland. Any claim that Ireland's history in the nineteenth and early twentieth centuries was especially turbulent or deprived, does not stand up to comparison with other countries in Europe. Historian Liam Kennedy has argued that: 'Whether it is location, climate, land occupancy, political and religious rights, economic welfare or violence, the Irish record is no worse than the modal European experience, and in a variety of respects more fortunate.'[6]

For most societies in Western Europe, including both parts of Ireland, the period between the late nineteenth and the early twentieth century was a crucial turning point in their history. The political systems and divisions which emerged at this stage, when, for the first time, modern political parties appeared, the majority of people could read and write, and the mass of the population could vote, proved very important for our modern world.[7] In what became Northern Ireland, politics emerged around divisions over two matters, religion and nationalism. Such political conflict was not unique. For example, Holland and Switzerland also faced divisions over religion while Italy and Norway experienced divisions over national unity. What was special about Northern Ireland was the way in which the national division and the political division linked and reinforced each other – nearly all protestants were unionists and nearly all catholics were nationalists. The important historical time for Northern Ireland was not 1169 or 1690, but the years 1885–1921.[8] These decades were also critical for determining the shape of modern politics in what became the Irish Republic, although this formative period was extended by another two years, due to the civil war.

If events between 1885 and 1921 established the nature of political divisions in Northern Ireland, the half century after 1921 witnessed the failure of society and government to cope successfully with the major problems which it faced. The existence of a protestant unionist majority and a catholic nationalist minority meant that under a system of Westminster majoritarian democracy the protestants dominated political power and society in general. Unionists won all the general elections, which, as the Ulster unionist leader, David Trimble, declared in Washington in March 1999, was 'fine for us but not so fine for other people'.[9] Along with the absence of real political influence for nationalists went inequalities in cultural, economic and social areas. In spite of the many achievements of the Northern Ireland government, there was failure to build a stable political system which could enjoy widespread support. The main challenge now for people in Northern Ireland is to create a form of government and society which has the allegiance of all its citizens, unionist and nationalist, catholic and protestant. The difficulty of achieving such an arrangement in the present moment is where the real problem lies, and not in the distant past.

Clearly, history is important for Northern Ireland, but no more so than elsewhere. Although it can be argued that all historical periods are of consequence for our modern world, it seems fair to claim that the last century is of special significance. It must be said, however, that both the last 100 years and the earlier history of Ireland are viewed by many as more important for today than historical developments or events for elsewhere. It is believed by many, inside and outside Northern Ireland, that history in Northern Ireland is uniquely significant. Because of this, ideas about the past take on a pressing importance and relevance. Often these views of the past are selective or based on myths. Nonetheless, the perceived sense of history which communities possess is very influential. Other societies refer to and use history but rarely to the extent found in Northern Ireland. The past is no more important here than elsewhere but people believe that it is, and that gives it a special role. Views of the past, therefore, are a powerful dynamic in Northern Ireland.

II

The formal educational system has played little direct part in the sense of history held by the main groups in Northern Ireland. In the nineteenth and early twentieth centuries there was very limited teaching of Irish history in primary or secondary schools because it was perceived as contentious and divisive. After 1921 Irish history was given an important role in the curriculum of schools in the Irish Free State as part of an effort to inculcate a strong sense of national identity in children: notes for teachers first issued in the 1930s stressed 'the continuity of the separatist idea from Tone to Pearse'.[10] Post-1921 in Northern Ireland the favoured course of action continued to be the downplaying of Irish history. History was reduced to a limited place in the school curriculum and Irish history was a very minor part of this. A school textbook, D.A. Chart's *History of Northern Ireland*, produced in 1927, omitted all reference to ' recent controversies' and indeed all political events since the union.[11]

This educational policy had an indirect effect on the sense of history which the communities acquired. Because of the lack of Irish history in the schools, people picked up knowledge of their history from songs, popular historical accounts and legends.

Commemoration of anniversaries of historical personalities or events was another way in which a popular view of history was communicated to the population at large. Writing in 1976 the educationalist Jack Magee commented: 'The Irish, despite what outsiders believe, are not preoccupied with history but obsessed with divisive and largely sectarian mythologies, acquired largely outside school.'[12] By this stage in the 1970s the teaching of Irish history in schools in Northern Ireland had actually improved, but for many people their knowledge of history was still strongly influenced by sources outside the classroom.

The sense of history in the unionist and loyalist community is formed in a number of ways. In a press interview in February 1998, the Northern Ireland protestant playwright, 34-year-old Gary Mitchell said: 'We never learned Irish history at school, which was really strange. It was all English history geared towards the exams. We didn't even do 1798, even though, woops, Wolfe Tone and Henry Mc Cracken were protestants'.[13] Another writer, Robert Greacen, has recently described his sense of history growing up in the late 1920s and early 1930s:

I did not learn the protestant version of history from books, but by word of mouth passed on from generation to generation. Ordinary folk like ourselves carried the facts – or alleged facts – of our history in our very bones and in our hearts. We were the people who had never surrendered and would never surrender. As each twelfth of July came around, protestant fervour would rise again and be reaffirmed.[14]

Each twelfth of July many members of the Orange Order celebrate the Battle of the Boyne when the Dutch protestant King William defeated the English catholic King James in 1690. Another key seventeenth-century date is 1688–9 when the city of Derry with its protestant defenders resisted siege by catholic forces. These are not just remote dates but are seen as critical for a sense of history held by many protestants which sees them facing siege and betrayal from that time to the present. The annual twelfth of July parades of the Orange Order and the twelfth of August parade in Derry of the Apprentice Boys of Derry serve to remind its members and others of the importance and relevance of these events. An editorial in the *Belfast Telegraph*, 12 July 1926, declared to readers that 'the occurrences of the years 1688 to 1690 were to a great extent parallel to those of recent times'. A speaker on a twelfth platform in 1993 declared: 'Two hundred years on, history is repeating itself all over the province and again the attack of republicanism focuses on Portadown as in 1795. We cannot ignore our history as some people would like us to do. We cannot forget the burning of protestants in Loughgall, the driving of protestants into the river Bann at Portadown...'[15]

These historical events have not always enjoyed such significance. One hundred years after the Boyne there were virtually no celebrations of the event in Ulster while the centenary parade to mark the relief of the city of Derry included the catholic bishop and clergy. By the last decades of the nineteenth century, however, with the rise of conflict between unionist and nationalist and protestant and catholic in its modern form, this events became very popular among the unionist and protestant community.[16] This view of protestant history is selective and contains various myths. It ignores those periods when protestants were not greatly concerned about such events, when they were divided and when they co-operated with catholics, as in the United Irishmen and the land reform movement. Nonetheless, this selective historical perspective is important for many unionists today. Unionists often talk of the 'age-old enemy' or 'Ulster's traditional enemies'.

A number of references were made during the debate in parliament on the Anglo-Irish Agreement in 1985.[17] Ian Paisley declared: 'Anyone who has read history should understand that this did not start in 1920, but goes back into the dim and distant past. There have been continued efforts to destroy the British presence in Ireland.' Peter Robinson read from Rudyard Kipling's 'Ulster 1912' and quoted Wilfrid Spender on Ulster bravery and sacrifices at the Somme, while Harold McCusker reminded members of how the Irish state had reneged on its 1925 agreement concerning the status of Northern Ireland. In recent decades unionist politicians have referred also to the actions of earlier unionist leaders, James Craig and Edward Carson.[18] Besides this emphasis on certain key events and personalities of the last four hundred years, some unionists, influenced by the writings of Dr Ian Adamson on the Cruithin people of ancient Ulster, have seen importance in earlier historical periods.[19]

For loyalist paramilitaries the past is also important. An observer in 1995 described how they seek the sanction of history as guardians of 'an inherited sacred trust, linked in direct succession to those of their forefathers who over and over again have barricaded themselves into their chosen territory and shouted defiance from where they stood with an ancestral gun in their hands'.[xx] Magazines associated with these groups carry articles not only about the Boyne and the siege of Derry from the seventeenth century and about the Battle of the Somme from the early twentieth century, but also about ancient Ulster. Cuchulainn, the ancient warrior of the *Tain Bo Cuailgne*, who became a nationalist folk hero in the nineteenth and early twentieth centuries, has recently been adopted as a loyalist folk hero. An article in the *New Ulster Defender*, in October 1993, declared that : 'Cuchulainn and the Red Branch Knights became renowned as the defenders of Ulster-defending Ulster against the men of Ireland. Many protestants in Ulster today are becoming aware of the feats of this great Ulster defender.'

Among nationalists and republicans there is also a strong sense of the past. This offers an historical account of a heroic Irish people who have suffered invasion and conquest but who have always survived. It ranges from early Celtic times to the Anglo-Norman invasion, the penal laws and the events of the Dublin Rising and aftermath, 1916–21. In this view, English and British intervention is seen as always detrimental to a people who have kept their catholic faith and political identity. In 1994 John Hume wrote of 'the traditional nationalist philosophy with which we all grew up. A philosophy that the essence of patriotism – *a la* 1916 – was the nobility of dying for Ireland and struggling against the British occupation of Ireland.'[21] Bernadette Devlin has declared: 'I learnt my history from my father, everything from the tales of the Tuatha De Dannan, and Celtic mythology to Larkin and Connolly.'[22]

Besides the influence of family and folk tales, this historical view is fostered by a range of other sources. Organisations, such the Ancient Order of Hibernians and the Irish National Foresters, often evoke historical scenes through their banners and parades, although not to the same extent as the Orange Order and the Apprentice Boys Clubs. [23] Many of the local Gaelic Athletic Association Clubs are named after Irish historical heroes. The principal G.A.A. playing grounds in Belfast, named Casement Park after Sir Roger Casement, were opened on 14 June 1953. On this occasion M.V. O'Donoghue, president of the G.A.A., included many historical references in his speech: 'The opening of this green field today is but the prelude to the final recovery of the fourth green field of Caitlin Ni Houlihan. [sic]. As long as Belfast holds such imperishable tabernacles of freedom as Cavehill and Casement Park, Belfast is Irish and Ulster is Ireland's.'[24] Although Irish history featured little on the pre-1970 syllabus, some catholic schools, in particular those run by the Christian brothers, taught history with a strong nationalist ethos.[25]

These historical views are not as deep rooted as is sometimes thought and in fact were greatly fostered by nationalist writers and groups of the nineteenth and twentieth centuries, such as the Young Irelanders in the 1840s and the Gaelic League in the 1890s and early 1900s. As with the popular history of the protestant and unionist community, so the popular history of the catholic and nationalist community contains myths and half-truths. This account leaves out those periods when Irish catholics did not pursue separatist goals, when they were divided among themselves and when they were aligned with protestants. For many constitutional nationalist politicians a sense of Irish history has often been important in their perspective on politics. In the debate on the Anglo-Irish Agreement in parliament in 1985, John Hume made reference to the events of 1912 and stated that 'the divisions in Ireland go back well beyond partition'. He also referred to the United Irishmen and C.S. Parnell.[26] In his speeches Hume often refers to traditional distrusts and our 'old quarrel.' Every day, the main northern catholic newspaper, the *Irish News*, carries a historical column beneath its editorial columns, usually recalling events between 1910 and 1930.

In the case of Sinn Féin and the I.R.A. there is plenty of evidence of the impact of the past. Republican magazines and newspapers such as *Iris* and *An Phoblacht* contain many historical articles on subjects such as the 1916 rising. A former I.R.A. volunteer, Shane O'Doherty, has described his reasons for joining the paramilitary organisation: 'It was the discovery of the tragedies of Irish history which first caused my desire to give myself to the I.R.A.' He recalled reading the writings of the executed leaders of 1916 and of earlier patriots: 'these writings ignited in me a passionate patriotism and an equally passionate desire to emulate the heroic deeds recounted therein'.[27] An editorial in *An Phoblacht*, on 15 April 1982, declared: 'We are confident that the I.R.A. stands ready and able, as the I.R.A. did in 1916.' Observers have commented frequently on the republican use of history. For example in 1993, journalist Dick Walsh wrote how I.R.A. members 'see themselves as a force apart, responding only to the commands of history'.[28]

These historical views have various effects on all sides. They give a selective, incomplete and often inaccurate picture to a community of its own history. They help to create distrust between people. The Mitchell commission of 1996 noted how because of the historical arguments about why the other side cannot be trusted 'even well-intentioned acts are often viewed with suspicion and hostility.'[29] Another major difficulty about these historical views which link the current situation to the remote past is that they create a sense of fatalism and continual confrontation which makes it difficult to achieve compromise and peaceful co-existence. Fascination with a supposedly unique history has obscured both the reality and opportunity to effectively confront the problem. Other European countries have faced these vexed matters over national identity and religion and have dealt with them better than has been the case in Northern Ireland. In their modern nineteenth and twentieth century histories countries such as Holland and Switzerland faced serious religious divisions while others like Norway and Italy experienced deep divisions over nationalism, but they have managed to cope with these problems.[30] Finally, these historical views have helped to legitimise violence. In his 1993 study of the 'troubles' J. Bowyer Bell observed that in other countries people were emboldened to act 'by Lenin's or Mao's example', but in Ireland the enemy was killed to 'history's tune and the blare of those unseen trumpets, audible always to the faithful'.[31]

III

Recent years have seen important changes in the ways that history and the past are used in, and about, Northern Ireland. In schools more Irish history is taught than before. Different historical traditions have been explored through the various programmes and projects of the Community Relations Council. Organisations such as Protestant and Catholic Encounter and church groups have run lectures and seminars to explore popular historical myths.[32] New popular histories, such as Jonathan Bardon's *A History of Ulster*, have given large numbers of the public a broader understanding of their past.[33] Reinterpretations in Irish history, with biographies like Marianne Elliott's *Wolfe Tone*, Tim Pat Coogan's *De Valera* and Alvin Jackson's *Sir Edward Carson*, has helped to undermine simplistic views of past heroes which are widely held, north and south.[34] There have been efforts over the last decade to see historical events and the commemorations which go with them in a broader and more inclusive way.[35] Since the early 1990s both unionist and nationalist politicians have been involved in Remembrance Day services in many places in Northern Ireland. On 8 October 1999 unionist-controlled Belfast City Council unveiled a memorial sculpture in the grounds of the city hall to honour James Magennis, the West Belfast catholic seaman and holder of the Victoria Cross. The bicentenary of the 1798 rebellion in Ireland was commemorated widely as a shared historical event.

In the Irish Republic the 1990s have seen a new effort to acknowledge the role of Irish servicemen in the two world wars. In 1995, at a ceremony at the Irish National War Memorial Park at Islandbridge in Dublin, attended by representatives of many political parties, including Tom Hartley of Sinn Féin, the taoiseach, John Bruton, acknowledged the involvement and sacrifices of Irish citizens in the British armed forces during the Second World War.[36] In 1998 President Mary McAleese and Queen Elizabeth II attended the opening of a memorial park at Mesen in Belgium in honour of Irish soldiers of the First World War.[37] In her speech on this occasion President McAleese declared:

> Those whom we commemorate here were doubly tragic. They fell victim to a war against oppression in Europe. Their memory, too, fell victim to a war for independence at home in Ireland...Respect for the memory of one set of heroes was often at the expense of respect for the memory of the other.[38]

From the early 1990s we can see evidence of the beginning of a different attitude to the importance of the past in political approach and speech. Sometimes this has involved an outright rejection of any role for history. After the murder by the I.R.A. of an alleged informer in south Armagh in July 1992, Dundalk priest Father John Duffy said: 'I could not believe that someone could be dumped on the roadside, naked, hooded and mutilated. If that is how you write Irish history then it is not worth giving to anyone'.[39] At other times it has involved an acknowledgement of the importance of history and an effort to draw either a different or more inclusive lesson from the past. These changes can be seen at government, party and popular level. They are apparent not only in Northern Ireland but also in London and Dublin. Indeed changes in attitude to historical matters in Great Britain and the Irish Republic are important for developments in Northern Ireland. At the same time many people, including some who have also taken this new approach, have continued to see events within the customary, historical framework discussed earlier. These varied and changing attitudes to history are evident if we survey some of the political documents and comments of the 1990s.

The Anglo-Irish Agreement of 1985 made no mention of history, but both the *Downing Street Joint Declaration* of 1993 and the *Frameworks for the future* document of 1995 carried important historical references.[40] Agreed on 15 December 1993, the *Downing Street Joint Declaration*, signed by John Major and Albert Reynolds, stated that the most important issue facing the people of Ireland, north and south, and the British and Irish governments together, was to 'remove the causes of conflict, to overcome the legacy of history and to heal the divisions which have resulted'. In paragraph 5, Albert Reynolds, on behalf of the Irish government, stated that 'the lessons of Irish history, and especially of Northern Ireland' show a political system will not work if it is rejected by a significant minority, and so he accepted that the consent of a majority of the people of Northern Ireland was required for a united Ireland.[41] The *Frameworks for the future* document of 22 February 1995 carried a foreword from John Major which declared that 'all parts of the community must find ways of living alongside each other without fear or antagonism. Age-old mistrusts need to be consigned to history.' [42] The 'new framework for agreement' paper in the document began by repeating the statement from the Downing Street Declaration about the need to remove the causes of conflict and to overcome the legacy of history. The paper went on to assert that:

> Both governments recognise that there is much for deep regret on all sides in the long and often tragic history of Anglo-Irish relations, and of relations in Ireland. They believe it is now time to lay aside, with dignity and forbearance, the mistakes of the past. A collective effort is needed to create, through agreement and reconciliation, a new beginning founded on consent, for relations within Northern Ireland, within the island of Ireland and between the peoples of these islands.

This new approach was reflected among politicians in the development of the peace process from the early 1990s. In a speech in Coleraine on 16 December, 1992, the secretary of state for Northern Ireland, Sir Patrick Mayhew, spoke about Britain's past role in Ireland and declared that 'there is much in the long and often tragic history of Ireland for deep regret, and the British government for its part shares in that regret to the full'.[43] In early February 1993, he spoke of helping the people of Northern Ireland to 'shake off the shackles of history'.[44] After a meeting in November

1992 between a unionist delegation and members of the Irish government, unionist M.P. Ken Maginnis remarked that 'the real dis-
appointment was that the Fianna Fáil party was caught by a large
1922 time warp. You only had to look at some of their papers to see
that sort of language.' He went on: 'there was no reality in terms of
1992 – there was no attempt to understand the unionist position'.[45]
In mid April 1993, however, in response to questions about changes
to articles two and three of the Irish constitution, Albert Reynolds,
the Fianna Fáil taoiseach, stated: 'We are not tied up in our past.
We want to move forward, to look at the changes required to ensure
that both communities can live together'.[46] In his address to the
Fianna Fáil Ard-Fheis on 6 November 1993, he acknowledged that
there was 'a more complex situation than existed during the independence struggle from 1916 to 1921.' He concluded that 'we must
not be prisoners of history' and that 'new patterns of co-operation
must transcend the antagonisms of a century between the two
political cultures'.[47] Other southern voices to echo this view included Dick Spring, the labour party leader, who in April and June of
1993 urged people to cast off 'the chains' and 'the baggage' of history.[48]

   In his New Year's message for 1993 Dr John Dunlop, moderator
of the presbyterian church, urged people in Northern Ireland not to
give up hope that their problems could be resolved. He described
the conflict as part of an historical process which stretched back
centuries, but expressed hope that the next chapter of this history
could be marked 'by cooperation instead of conflict'.[49] On 7 March
1993, in an article in the *Sunday Times*, he wrote:

> Protestants talk of siege and survival. For most unionists, the siege of
> Derry and the Battle of the Boyne only continue as powerful symbols
> from the past because they speak of the periodic and constantly
> renewed threats of being overwhelmed by the Irish majority, whether in
> 1641, 1690, 1798, the home rule crisis of the early 1920s or in the vio-
> lence of the present.[50]

Dunlop warned that ' the trouble with the siege mentality is that
it leads to defensive thinking, which often does not have the

flexibility or generosity of spirit to discern where its own self inter-
est lies, never mind the legitimate interests of other people'.
Another historical perspective was expressed by Ian Paisley in late
October 1993, when he attacked talks between John Hume and
Gerry Adams, accusing Hume of trying to sell the people of the
province 'like cattle on the hoof to their traditional enemies.'

Criticism of the I.R.A. campaign also made use of historical
images. In mid February 1993, in a sermon in west Belfast at the
funeral of an alleged informer who had been murdered by the
I.R.A., Father Aidan Denny stated:

> Chris Harte was murdered by his fellow Irishmen in the name of patri-
> otism. Republicans must ask themselves, what would Patrick Pearse or
> James Connolly have to say today? If Bobby Sands were alive, would he
> say it was worth while giving up his life for this? It is utter madness.
> Does no-one realise that it is utter madness.[51]

In March, Seamus Mallon, of the S.D.L.P., accused the republican
movement of being 'weighed down by history,' while in April a
South African journalist, Rian Malan described them as 'so steeped
in ancestral memories of martyrdom that they can't see straight any
more'.[52] An I.R.A. statement of 8 April 1993 declared that 'the root
cause of this conflict is the historic and ongoing violent denial of
Irish national rights'.[53] In an interview in early October1993, however, Gerry Adams, the Sinn Féin leader, acknowledged change in
the republican movement: 'we have adopted a different approach
which is more in keeping with the reality of Ireland in 1993 than
perhaps harking back to Ireland in 1918'.[54] On the B.B.C. programme *Spotlight* on 21 October 1993, John Hume, the S.D.L.P.
leader, spoke of the 'distrust of others based on the past,' and argued
that now was the time to leave the past.

Following the *Downing Street Declaration* of December 1993 we
find continued references to the past and how it should be dealt
with. On 4 January 1994 John Hume welcomed the *Downing Street
Declaration* and stated:

> As we face the twenty-first century, surely the time has come to leave

the past behind us. Our present has been created by the past and it is not all that pleasant. The time has come to leave it behind and to look to the future.[55]

He returned to this theme a number of times during the year, calling on the I.R.A. to renounce violence and on unionists to 'leave their past attitude behind them.'[56] Republicans were more reserved initially about the *Downing Street Declaration* for various reasons. One reason expressed by Gerry Adams was that 'we are dealing with centuries of history'.[57] At the same time, Sinn Féin councillor Tom Hartley explained that 'modern republican ideology, while rooted in history, is above all the result of a 25-year learning process which began with the civil rights campaign....'[58] At the end of August 1994 the I.R.A. declared a ceasefire in a statement which did not dwell on the past, but did refer briefly to all those 'who had died for Irish freedom'.[59] The *Irish News* editorial, appearing the day after the ceasefire, saw this announcement in the 'tradition of Patrick Pearce's noble decision to lay down arms after the Easter Rising of 1916'.[60] The ceasefire declaration of October from the loyalist groups carried no reference to the past beyond the recent troubles. We may note, however, that their declaration was made at Fernhill House, a building with historic links with the original U.V.F.[61]

The period between the publication of the *Frameworks* document of February 1995 and of the *Belfast Agreement* of April 1998 saw continued reference to history in various ways. At government level there was mention both of the past and of the need to deal with or leave the past behind. Secretary of State for Northern Ireland, Sir Patrick Mayhew, spoke in September 1995 of the government's desire for a 'political settlement to the ancient difficulties of Ireland' and in July 1996 of the difficulties of a process which is intended 'to overcome divisions which go back centuries'.[62] In December 1995 prime minister John Major regretted poor Anglo-Irish relations in the recent past: 'I think the reason for that is locked in history. It ought to remain in history and we ought to take advantage of the bilateral opportunities that occur'.[63] In reference to Northern Ireland, President Bill Clinton spoke of how on his trip to Belfast in November 1995 he had seen optimism 'in the faces of two communities, divided by bitter history', while in his St Patrick's Day message of March 1996 he stated: 'We must not permit the process of reconciliation in Northern Ireland to be destroyed by those who are blinded by the hatreds of the past'.[64]

The difficulties of dealing with the past were highlighted in two reports during these years, covering the contentious issues of parades and of decommissioning of arms. The report of the international body on decommissioning, chaired by Senator George Mitchell, and issued in January 1996, stressed the problem of the absence of trust for progress on this matter:

> Common to many of our meetings were arguments, steeped in history, as to why the other side cannot be trusted. As a consequence, even well-intentioned acts are often viewed with suspicion and hostility ...

> But a resolution of the decommissioning issue – or any other issue – will not be found if the parties resort to their vast inventories of historical recrimination or, as it was put to us several times, what is really needed is the decommissioning of mindsets in Northern Ireland.[65]

The report of the independent review of parades and marches, chaired by Peter North and published in January 1997, noted that 'remembering in Northern Ireland is complicated by opposing perspectives, by the long, lingering pain of remembered past suffering and conflict'. The report described how:

> We met representatives of the Loyal Orders who have recently suffered at the hands of the Provisional I.R.A. and who recall the deliverance of the protestant population in a battle which took place more than 300 years ago. Their catholic neighbours meantime remember the same battle as a defeat, along with their more recent experience of discrimination at the hands of unionist administration.[66]

Attitudes among the parties to this question of the past were mixed. In March 1995 David Ervine, leader of the Progressive Unionist Party urged unionists to 'break the myth and lay the ghosts' while in June 1995 Gary McMichael warned: 'I think in this society we have developed a very dangerous fashion of looking into history and using history as a weapon and a means of justifying actions that were taken'.[67] In August 1996 Cecil Walker, Ulster Unionist Party M.P. urged his political colleagues to 'scatter the historical cobwebs'.[68] Apart from this remark there has been little reference to forgetting the past among speeches of Ulster unionist M.P.s, but there has also been limited attempt to use it. In contrast, the Democratic Unionist party, in particular its leader, Ian Paisley, continues to refer to and draw lessons from the past. He often talks of Ulster's 'traditional enemies.'[69] At his party conference in November 1995 he warned that 'the spirit which inspired our forefathers to refuse to bow the knee to the enemies of liberty still burns in the breast of their sons and daughters.' He continued: 'At the Somme it was rightly said that the men of Ulster were lions but the English officers directing the battle were asses.'[70] In the same year Paisley was the co-author of a pamphlet on the history of Northern Ireland, including the 1641 massacres, the siege of Derry and the battle of the Boyne: it carried a warning that 'Ulster's history is today repeating itself.'[71]

Among members of the Social Democratic and Labour Party, in particular John Hume, there has been more reference to leaving the past behind. In December 1995, at the launch of a book on Daniel O'Connell, Hume stated: 'If there is a lesson from Daniel O'Connell it is – The aislings of our ancestors should inspire us, not control us'.[72] On 4 February 1998 he urged that: 'In learning the lessons of the past we must not become prisoners of the past – the major obstacle to success is the unwillingness of certain parties to leave the past behind them and their continued use of the language of the past'.[73] As regards Sinn Féin, we may note that at their ard fheis during these years the speeches of Gerry Adams made little reference to the past, apart from general statements, such as expressing the need to 'prepare this party to fulfil its historic responsibility in the time ahead'.[74] On other occasions, Sinn Féin spokesmen have referred to history. In December 1995 Sinn Féin chairman, Mitchel McLaughlin, declared: 'Any student of Irish history will, and can, verify what Gerry Adams and Martin McGuinness have been saying. Britain has not won a war. The I.R.A. has not surrendered. The conditions for peace are still present, but so are the conditions for renewed war'.[75]

The *Belfast Agreement*, reached after multi-party negotiations which concluded on 10 April 1998, made little mention of history or the past. It began with a declaration of support which referred to the participants' belief that the agreement offered 'a truly historic opportunity for a new beginning' and stated that 'the tragedies of the past' had left a deep legacy of suffering in all the deaths and injuries, but otherwise made no reference to history. Much of the reaction to the agreement, however, saw it as part of a long term historical picture. The *Irish Times* website on the agreement had an historical introduction which began with the Anglo-Norman invasion of 1169, although an editorial of 11 April referred to peacemakers who 'buried the quarrel of 400 years'.[76] An editorial in the *Belfast Telegraph* on 21 May talked of a 'new partnership between the peoples of these islands, British and Irish, that will replace 800 years of enmity with trust and friendship'.[77] On the eve of the signing of the agreement, prime minister Tony Blair declared: 'I feel the hand of history upon our shoulders. I really do'.[78] In September 1998, President Bill Clinton, in an indirect compliment to the agreement, praised the progress of Northern Ireland's peace process as helping the whole world awaken from history's nightmares' by showing that 'ancient enmities' could be overcome'. He went on to claim that if the process was successfully concluded then this example could be shown to conflict areas in the Middle East, the Aegean, the Indian sub-continent and in the tribal strife of Africa'.[79]

IV

The historical perspective expressed above on the *Belfast Agreement* is one that many would agree with. The view that the conflict in Northern Ireland is the outcome of four or eight hundred years of enmity has wide acceptance, both within Northern Ireland and outside, although people would differ as to whether or not the conflict is now being resolved. It has been argued here, however, that this view is neither valid nor helpful. Northern Ireland faces modern day problems to do with serious divisions over religion and nationality, which other societies have also faced in the modern period, some successfully and some not. The conflict, therefore, is not to do with ancient enmities but with contemporary difficulties and failures. For Northern Ireland, as for most other European countries, the last hundred years have been important. The political system and society established at the end of the nineteenth and the beginning of the twentieth century proved unable to achieve a stable consensus of support from its citizens. The *Belfast Agreement* has set down new parameters for relations between the conflicting groups in Northern Ireland, between Northern Ireland and the Irish Republic and between the Irish Republic and the U.K. These arrangements are a modern attempt to deal with very real contemporary conflicts and divisions. This view of history is also damaging because emphasis on a perceived sense of age old animosity makes it more difficult for such new political arrangements to work.

In his speech of 8 September 1998, President Clinton argued that success in the peace process in Northern Ireland where there had been 'conflicts for hundreds of years' would have lessons for other societies faced with 'ancient enmities'. Closer examination, however, of some of the areas which he mentioned show that while their conflicts are often blamed on age-old animosities, this is usually not the main cause. Their problems relate primarily to the failure of twentieth century political systems to deal with religious and ethnic divisions, but perceptions or myths of history have come to play a part in these places. In Rwanda, for example, where the conflict has been blamed on 'ancient tribal hatreds' the real problem lay with the political arrangements established in the 1960s by the outgoing colonial power which one group then exploited. Distortions of history, 'firmly held but mistaken ideas of the Rwandan past', creating a sense of ancient conflict, served to heighten tension but was not the cause of it.[80] In the former Yugoslavia, the main cause of the current problems lies in the make up of the state and structures established in 1921, the impact of Nazi intervention and the impact of Tito's regime and its collapse. The on-going conflict here between the different groups is often expressed in historical terms,

but historians have pointed to the many myths and half truths contained in these stories of ancient ethnic hatreds. As one commentator has remarked about the situation in Kosovo, the conflict was not an 'inevitable working out of immemorial animosities', but 'a twentieth century response to twentieth century conditions'.[81] The important lesson to be taken from Northern Ireland is that it is necessary to create a society and system of government which can win the allegiance of the different groups. At the same time perceptions of 'ancient enmities' should be challenged and not allowed to unduly influence the agenda.

While history is not the cause of the problem in Northern Ireland, perceptions of that history are of considerable influence. Strong views of history are held by many in the various communities in Northern Ireland. These views are often selective, contain myths and have changed over the years. People use history to justify their positions and influence their actions. In some ways this is positive in that it gives a sense of identity and purpose that can bind a community. In other ways, however, it is harmful. In Northern Ireland it has helped to create a fatalistic sense of continuous conflict that undermines trust between communities and makes a resolution of religion and nationality more difficult. Changes in recent years to historical attitudes have helped to challenge exclusive and selective views of history at large. Many today reject these ideas about 'ancient enmities' and are willing to examine myths involved in the popular views of history of their own communities. New approaches to commemoration of events such as 1798 and Remembrance Day have helped to emphasise shared history. There is an awareness of how history has been used to create exclusive and sectarian identities. At different levels there have been attempts to present a wider sense of history which shows how all sides have been effected. These changes are of importance for the political scene. The current peace process has been helped by this new approach. It has lead many to try to deal with modern problems in a contemporary rather than an historical setting. It has caused some to urge a complete break with the perceived past and others to see historical matters in a broader and more inclusive way. Erosion of the idea of continual conflict back to early history has helped to remove some of the distrust and hostility which has existed. Serious difficulties remain over vital issues in Northern Ireland, but for many involved these changes allow such matters to be dealt with in their own right, uninfluenced by the 'baggage of history'.

NOTES

CHAPTER 1

1 Aiken McClelland, *William Johnston of Ballykilbeg* (Lurgan, 1990), p. 69.

2 Jonathan Bardon, *A History of Ulster* (Belfast, 1992), p. 158.

3 Anthony Buckley, 'Uses of history among Ulster protestants' in Gerald Dawe and J.W. Foster (eds), *The poet's place: Ulster literature and society* (Belfast, 1991), p. 262.

4 David McKittrick, *Despatches from Belfast* (Belfast, 1989), p. 29.

5 A.T.Q. Stewart, *The narrow ground: the roots of conflict in Ulster* (London, 1977; revised edition, London, 1989).

6 T.G. Fraser, 'The siege: its history and legacy, 1688–1889' in M.G.R. O'Brien (ed.), *Derry/Londonderry: history and society* (Dublin, 1998) and T.G. Fraser, 'The Apprentice Boys and the relief of Derry parades' in T.G. Fraser (ed.), *The Irish parading tradition: following the drum* (London, 2000), pp 173–90. See also Desmond Murphy, *Derry, Donegal and modern Ulster, 1790–1921* (Derry, 1981).

7 Sam Burnside, 'No temporising with the foe: literary materials relating to the siege and relief of Derry' in *The Linen Hall Review*, vol. 5, no. 3 (Autumn, 1988), pp 4–9.

8 Ian McBride, *The siege of Derry in Ulster protestant mythology* (Dublin, 1997).

9 C.D. Milligan, *The Walker Club centenary, 1844–1944, with an historical record of the Apprentice Boys and bibliographical notes on Governor Walker* (Derry, 1944); *The Murray Club centenary 1847–1947: a hundred years of history of the Murray Club of Apprentice Boys of Derry, with the story of Murray's part in the defence of Derry in 1689* (Derry, 1947); *Browning memorials (with a short historical note on the rise and progress of the Apprentice Boys of Derry Clubs)* (Derry, 1952); *The centenary of the revival of the Mitchelburne Club, 1854–1954* (Derry, 1954). For their assistance in obtaining copies of these publications I am very grateful to Billy Coulter and Tony Crowe.

10 Quoted in John Hempton (ed.) *Siege and history of Londonderry* (Derry, 1861), p. 41.

11 See McBride, *Siege of Derry in mythology*, p. 36.

12 Ibid., pp 24–7.

13 Hempton, *Siege*, pp 415–7.

14 Milligan, *Browning memorials*, p. 9.

15 Hempton, *Siege*, pp 77–88.

[16] Brian Lacy, *Siege City: the story of Derry and Londonderry* (Belfast, 1990), pp 154–8.

[17] McBride, *Siege of Derry in mythology*, p. 14.

[18] Hempton, *Siege*, pp 436–48; McBride, *Siege of Derry in mythology*, p. 48.

[19] Milligan, *Walker Club*, p. 20

[20] McBride, *Siege of Derry in mythology*, pp 46–52.

[21] *Apprentice Boys of Derry, list of members, 1879* (Dublin, 1879).

[22] *Ordnance survey of the county of Londonderry, vol.1: city and north western liberties of Londonderry, parish of Templemore* (Dublin, 1837), p. 198. Published in 1837, this comment probably refers to the situation before the founding of the Apprentice Boys of Derry Club in 1835.

[23] *Report of the commissioners of inquiry, into the riots and disturbances in the city of Londonderry, 1869*, H.C. 1870 (C.35), xiv, p. 207. Rules and byelaws of the Apprentice Boys of Derry Club, formed 1835.

[24] *Londonderry Sentinel*, 22 Dec. 1838. For an interesting 1830s depiction of the burning of Lundy see the print in the section of plates in W.E. Vaughan (ed.) *A new history of Ireland: vol. v. Ireland under the union* (Oxford, 1989).

[25] Milligan, *Walker Club* p. 40.

[26] *Londonderry Sentinel*, 17 Aug. 1839.

[27] McBride, *Siege of Derry in mythology*, p. 49; *Official tercentenary brochure*, pp 21–8.

[28] Ibid., p. 45.

[29] *Rules of commissioners, 1869: rules of Apprentice Boy of Derry Club*, pp 180, 195.

[30] Ibid., p. 107.

[31] McClelland, *Johnston*, p. 71.

[32] *Northern Whig*, 13 Aug. 1867.

[33] McClelland, *Johnston*, p. 71.

[34] F.J. Porter, *Be in earnest: a sermon delivered by Rev. F.J. Porter before the Mitchelburn Club on 12 Aug. 1863* (Derry, 1863), p. 21; *Report of Commissioners, 1869*, p. 180.

[35] *Belfast News Letter*, 14 Aug. 1877.

[36] Milligan, *Murray Club*, p. 5.

[37] *Londonderry Sentinel*, 13 Aug. 1877.

[38] *Report of commissioners, 1869*, pp 180, 195. Letter from J.G. Ferguson, governor of the Apprentice Boys, 7 Dec. 1867, in David Miller, *Still under siege* (Lurgan, 1989), p. 70. Report on 1870 parade from *Northern Whig*, 13 Aug. 1870.

[39] *Official tercentenary brochure* p. 36.

[40] *Londonderry Sentinel*, 13 Aug. 1889.

[41] Ibid.

[42] McClelland, *Johnston*.

[43] *Report of commissioners, 1869,* pp 192, 195.

[44] J.S. Crawford, *Alleluia: the commemoration service, preached on 12th Aug. 1864, the 175th anniversary of the relief of Londonderry, in the Strand Road Presbyterian Church* (Derry, 1864).

[45] See B.M. Walker, *Ulster politics: the formative years, 1868–86* (Belfast, 1989).

[46] *Northern Whig,* 13 Aug. 1889. A review of Philip Dwyer (ed.) *The siege of Londonderry* (London, 1893) in the presbyterian weekly *The Witness,* 16 Nov. 1893, was highly critical of the depiction of Walker's role in the siege: 'how he got the monument on Derry's walls surpasses everything'.

[47] *Belfast News Letter,* 20 Dec. 1855; *Belfast Telegraph,* 13 Aug. 1873; *Northern Whig,* 20 Dec. 1886.

[48] *Belfast News Letter,* 13 Aug. 1975.

[49] *Impartial Reporter,* 14 Aug. 1845; *Londonderry Sentinel,* 17 Aug. 1849; *Impartial Reporter,* 15 Aug. 1872, 14 Aug. 1879, 16 Aug. 1888.

[50] *Belfast News Letter,* 13 Aug. 1889, 14 Aug. 1889.

[51] Ibid., 14 Aug. 1889.

[52] *Londonderry Sentinel,* 13 Aug. 1889.

[53] Ibid., 14 Aug. 1900.

[54] *Belfast News Letter,* 13 Aug. 1914.

[55] Ibid., 13 Aug. 1912.

[56] *Londonderry Sentinel,* 19 Dec. 1912.

[57] Milligan, *Murray,* pp 38–41.

[58] *For God and Ulster: an alternative guide to the loyal orders* (Derry, 1997), p. 14.

[59] *Official tercentenary brochure,* p. 4.

[60] *Londonderry Sentinel,* 14 Aug. 1923.

[61] *Northern Whig,* 13 Aug. 1924.

[62] Ibid., 13 Aug. 1924; *Londonderry Sentinel,* 14 Aug. 1930, 13 Aug. 1936.

[63] *Londonderry Sentinel,* 15 Aug. 1939.

[64] Ibid., 14 Aug. 1923.

[65] Ibid., 14 Aug. 1930.

[66] Ibid., 15 Aug. 1939.

[67] Ibid.

[68] *Official tercentenary brochure,* p. 38.

[69] *Londonderry Sentinel,* 15 Aug. 1939.

[70] *Official tercentenary brochure,* p. 38.

[71] Although the tercentenary brochure suggests that Easter parades started in 1925, this is not confirmed by press reports.

[72] *Londonderry Sentinel,* 13 Aug. 1936.

[73] Milligan, *Murray Club,* p. 45.

[74] *Londonderry Sentinel,* 20 Dec. 1938.

[75] Ibid., 15 Aug. 1939.

[76] Ibid.

77 Ibid.

78 *Belfast News Letter*, 13 and 14 Aug. 1889, 14 Aug. 1900.

79 Ibid., 13 Aug. 1910; *Armagh Guardian*, 13 Aug. 1910.

80 *Belfast News Letter*, 13 Aug. 1923; *Northern Whig*, 13 Aug. 1930.

81 Aiken McClelland, 'The Orange Order in Co. Monaghan' in *Clogher Record* (1978), p. 387.

82 *Belfast News Letter*, 13 Aug. 1939. These are instances of Black perceptories from Down and Antrim attending these 12 August commemorations in south Ulster or in their own counties in the 1920s and 1930s but they are few.

83 *Junior Orange Association of Ireland, Belfast County Lodge, 1925–75* (Belfast, 1975).

84 David Fitzpatrick, *The two Irelands, 1912–39* (Oxford, 1998), p. 178.

85 W.C. Trimble, *The history of Enniskillen: with references to some manors in Co. Fermanagh*, vol. III, (Enniskillen, 1921), pp 77–89.

86 *Londonderry Sentinel*, 13 Aug. 1946 (nearly 3,000); *Northern Whig*, 13 Aug. 1946 (2,500).

87 Ibid., 13 Aug. 1946.

88 *Belfast News Letter*, 13 Aug. 1947.

89 *Northern Whig*, 15 Aug. 1949, 13. Aug. 1951, 11 Aug. 1952; *Londonderry Sentinel*, 13 Aug. 1957, 13 Aug. 1958.

90 Ibid., 15 Aug. 1957, 13 Aug. 1958.

91 Ibid., 12 Aug. 1946 (over 7,000); ibid., 13 Aug. 1947 (6,000); *Belfast News Letter*, 13. Aug. 1957 (8,000); *Londonderry Sentinel*, 19 Aug. 1959 (5,000). On 13 Aug. 1946, the *Londonderry Sentinel* reported that over 12,000 Apprentice Boys attended the parade but this is probably exaggerated.

92 *Londonderry Sentinel*, 15 Aug. 1950 (40,000); ibid., 13 Aug. 1953 (30,000).

93 *Official tercentenary brochure*, pp 37–42.

94 W.J. Wallace, *Browning Club Apprentice Boys of Derry*, (Derry, 1961), p. 37.

95 *Official tercentenary brochure*, p. 37.

96 *Londonderry Sentinel*, 15 Aug. 1962, 19 Aug. 1964.

97 Ibid., 22 Dec. 1964.

98 Ibid., 19 Aug. 1964.

99 *Ulster Unionist Council Yearbook, 1966* (Belfast, 1966).

100 *Apprentice Boys of Derry, members ticket*, 1971 (Dungannon, 1971). I am grateful to Tom Fraser for drawing my attention to this list, a copy of which can be found in the Linen Hall Library, Belfast.

101 Ibid., 15 Aug. 1979; *Belfast Telegraph*, 13 Aug. 1985; *Londonderry Sentinel*, 18 Aug., 22 Dec. 1982.

102 Ibid., 16 Aug. 1972; *Belfast Telegraph*, 12 Aug. 1985.

103 *Londonderry Sentinel*, 17 Aug. 1977; *Belfast News Letter*, 15 Aug. 1988; General–Secretary Derek Miller put total membership at 11,000 in 1988,

Belfast Telegraph, 15 Aug. 1988; a figure of 12,000 is given in the *Official tercentenary brochure*, p. 37.

104 *Londonderry Sentinel*, 17 Aug. 1977, 10 Aug. 1989, 15 Aug. 1988.

105 *Apprentice Boys of Derry, member's ticket 1971(Dungannon, 1971).*

106 *Londonderry Sentinel*, 18 Aug. 1982.

107 Ibid., 16 Aug. 1989.

108 Ibid.

109 *Official tercentenary brochure*, p. 3.

110 Peter Robinson, *Their cry was 'no surrender': an account of the siege of Londonderry, 1688–9* (Belfast, 1988), pp 17–18.

111 Neil Jarman, *Material conflicts: parades and visual displays in Northern Ireland* (Oxford, 1997).

112 *Londonderry Sentinel*, 13 Aug. 1939.

113 Eric Hobsbawm, 'Inventing traditions' in Eric Hobsbawm and Terence Ranger (eds) *The invention of tradition* (Cambridge 1983; 1995 reprint), pp 1–14.

CHAPTER 2

1 *Irish Times*, 9 Sept. 1998.

2 Father Walter Forde (ed.), *From heritage to hope: Christian perspectives on the 1798 bicentenary* (Gorey, Co. Wexford, 1998).

3 See Peter Collins, 'The contest of memory: the continuing impact of 1798 commemorations' in *Eire Ireland*, vol. xxxiv, no. 2, (Summer,1999), pp 48–50.

4 Sir Roger Casement to Jack Kelly, quoted in *Irish Times*, 12 Aug. 1999.

5 *Irish Times*, 4 Dec. 1998.

6 Marianne Elliott, *Wolfe Tone: the prophet of Irish independence* (New Haven,1989), p. 411; profile of Tone by John Burns, *Sunday Times*, 24 Jan. 1999.

7 Elliott, *Wolfe Tone*, Introduction.

8 D.J. Gahan, *The people's rising, Wexford 1798* (Dublin, 1995), pp 299–300.

9 Marianne Elliott, *Partners in revolution: the United Irishmen and France* (Yale, 1982), pp 340–9.

10 Sean Connolly, 'Aftermath and adjustment' in W.E. Vaughan (ed.), *A new history of Ireland, Vol. V Ireland under the union, 1801–70* (Oxford, 1989) pp 10–20.

11 John Devoy, *Recollections of an Irish rebel* (New York, 1929; Shannon, 1969), p. 7.

12 Kevin Whelan, *The tree of liberty: radicalism, catholicism and the construction of Irish identity* (Cork, 1996), pp 171–2.

13 Quoted by Diarmuid Ferriter, 'Aftermath and legacy of '98', *Irish Independent*, 23 May 1999.

14 Quoted by Thomas Pakenham, *The year of liberty: the story of the great Irish rebellion of 1798* (London,1969: revised edition, London, 1997), p. 348.

[15] 'Memorials of Wexford' in Thomas Davis, *Literary and historical essays* (New York, 1868), p. 107.

[16] John Finigan (ed.), *The prison journal of Anne Devlin* (Cork, 1968), pp 118–23.

[17] See Elliott, *Partners in revolution,* p. 367.

[18] See illustration in Myrtle Hill, Brian Turner and Kenneth Dawson (eds), *1798 rebellion in Co. Down* (Newtownards,1998), p. 115.

[19] R.B. McDowell, *Public opinion and government policy in Ireland, 1801–46* (London,1952), p. 50.

[20] Elliott, *Partners in revolution,* p. 342.

[21] Ibid., p. 342; Connolly, *Aftermath,* pp 19–20.

[22] *Ordnance survey memoirs of Ireland: parishes of Co. Antrim,* xiii, *Templepatrick and district,* vol. 35 (Belfast, 1996), p. 123.

[23] R.F. Holmes, *Henry Cooke* (Belfast,1981), pp 4–5. Holmes points out that presbyterian historians in the late nineteenth century, such as Thomas Witherow, tried to minimise the violence of the rebellion, but evidence confirms that Cooke's home area experienced considerable violence during 1798.

[24] R.F. Holmes, *Our presbyterian heritage* (Belfast,1985), p. 108.

[25] Quoted in Holmes, *Cooke,* p. 5.

[26] R.M. Young (ed.), *Historical notices of old Belfast* (Belfast, 1896), p.192.

[27] Charles Gavan Duffy, *My life in two hemispheres, vol.1,* (London,1898; Shannon,1969), pp 61–3.

[28] See M.H. Thuente, *The harp restrung: the United Irishmen and the rise of Irish literary nationalism* (Syracuse, 1994) pp 193–4.

[29] For a lengthy discussion see Whelan, *Tree of liberty,* pp 133–75.

[30] Sir Richard Musgrave, *Memoirs of the different rebellions in Ireland from the arrival of the English* (third edition, Dublin,1802), pp viii–vi.

[31] W.H. Maxwell, *History of the rebellion in 1798* (London, 1845: new edition, London,1891), npp 1–13, 316–29, 433.

[32] Whelan, *Tree of liberty,* pp 149–50, 159–60.

[33] Martin Burke, 'Piecing together a shattered past: the historical writings of the United Irish exiles in America' in David Dickson, Daire Keogh and Kevin Whelan (eds), *The United Irishmen: republicanism, radicalism and rebellion* (Dublin, 1993) pp 297–306.

[34] *Life of Theobald Wolfe Tone, founder of the United Irish Society, and adjutant general and chef de brigade in the service of the French and Bavarian republics. Written by himself and continued by his son; with his political writings and fragments of his diary, 2 vols* (Washington, 1826).

[35] See Thomas Bartlett (ed.), *Life of Theobald Wolfe Tone* (Dublin, 1998), pp xli–xlvi.

[36] R.R. Madden, *The United Irishmen, their lives and times,* 3 series, 7 volumes (London, 1842–5).

[37] Ibid., vol.1, p.xii.

38 T.L. Birch, *A letter from an Irish emigrant to his friend in the United States giving an account of the commotions of the United Irishmen and Orange societies, and of several battles and military executions* (Philadelphia, 1799); Samuel Neilson, *Brief statement of a negotiation between certain United Irishmen and the Irish government in July, 1798* (New York, 1802).

39 William Steele Dickson, *A narrative of the confinement of William Steel Dickson* (Dublin, 1812).

40 Charles Dickson, *Revolt in the north* (Dublin,1960; London, 1997), pp 184–9; W.D. Bailie, 'Presbyterian clergymen and the County Down rebellion of 1798' in Myrtle Hill, Brian Turner and Kenneth Dawson (eds), *1798: rebellion in County Down* (Newtownards, 1998), pp 163–7.

41 *Belfast Magazine*, vol. 1,1825, pp 56–64, 540–8; *Ulster Monthly Magazine*, no.1 (Jan.1830).

42 C.H. Teeling, *Personal narrative of the Irish rebellion of 1798* (London, 1828).

43 W.H. Drummond (ed.), *Autobiography of Archibald Hamilton Rowan* (Dublin, 1840); P.T. Orr, 'Doing history: a re-interpretation of the life of the United Irishman Archibald Hamilton Rowan (1751–1834)' in Hill, Turner and Dawson, *1798 in Down*, pp 211–30.

44 Quoted in Horace Reid, 'The battle of Ballynahinch: an anthology of the documents' in Hill, Turner and Dawson, *1798 in Down*, p. 134.

45 George Benn, *The history of the town of Belfast* (Belfast, 1823).

46 *Down Recorder*, 9 June 1838.

47 S.L. Corrigan, *A new and improved history of the rebellion in Ireland in the year 1798, abridged from the most authentic sources, with an appendix, containing a history of the Orange Association* (Belfast, 1844).

48 Samuel McSkimin, *Annals of Ulster-Ireland fifty years ago* (Belfast, 1849). Before his death Mc Skimin was used as an important source of information by a number of historians including R.R. Madden.

49 G.K. Peatling, 'Who fears to speak of politics? John Kells Ingram and hypothetical nationalism' in *Irish Historical Studies*, vol.xxxi, no. 122 (Nov. 1998), pp 202–4. Sean Barrett, 'John Kells Ingram (1823–1907)', Trinity Economic Paper, no. 9, 1999.

50 Thuente, *The harp restrung*, pp193–230.

51 Richard Davis, *The Young Ireland movement* (Dublin, 1987), pp 171–257. Sean Ryder, 'Speaking of '98: Young Ireland and republican memory' in *Eire Ireland*, vol. xxxiv, no. 2 (Summer 1999), pp 51–69.

52 In 1782 patriots led by Henry Grattan in the Irish parliament, with the backing of the Irish Volunteers, achieved legislative independence for parliament, under the crown.

53 Thuente, *Harp restrung*, p. 212. Davis, *Young Ireland*, p. 222.

54 John Mitchel (ed.), *The poems of Thomas Davis* (New York, 1868).

55 C.J. Woods 'Tone's grave at Bodenstown: memorials and commemorations, 1798–1913' in Dorothea Siegmund-Schultze (ed.), *Irland: Gesellschaft und Kultur*-VI (Halle, 1989) pp 141–5.

56 Davis, *Young Ireland*, p. 243; P.S. O'Hegarty, *A history of Ireland under the union, 1801–1922* (London, 1952), p. 419; D.G. Boyce, *Nationalism in Ireland* (London,1982; second edition, London, 1991), pp 171–5.

57 Brendan Ó Cathaoir, 'The rising of 1848' in *History Ireland*, vol. 6, no. 3 (Autumn 1998), p. 26; Richard Davis, *Young Ireland*, pp 147–53; Boyce, *Nationalism*, pp 174–5.

58 Elliott, *Wolfe Tone*, p. 414.

59 John Mitchel, *An Ulsterman for Ireland* (reprint of his *Nation* letters), with introduction by Eoin MacNeill (Dublin, 1917), p. 29.

60 Boyce, *Nationalism*, p. 174.

61 See O Cathaoir, *Rising of 1848*, pp 26–8; Davis, *Young Ireland*, pp 159–62.

62 Carmel Heaney, 'William Smith O'Brien in Van Dieman's land' in *History Ireland*, vol. 6, no. 3 Autumn 1998), p.30.

63 T.W. Moody, 'Fenianism, home rule and the land war' in T.W. Moody and F.X. Martin (eds), *The course of Irish history* (Cork, 1967; revised edition, Cork, 1984), pp 278–80; R.V. Comerford, *The Fenians in context; Irish politics and society, 1848–82* (Dublin, 1985; new edition, Dublin,1998).

64 Devoy, *Recollections of an Irish rebel*, p. 6. John O'Leary also described Fenianism as the 'direct and, I think, inevitable outcome of '48, as '48 was the equally inevitable, if more indirect, outcome of '98'. T.W. Moody, *The Fenian movement* (Cork, 1968), p.102.

65 Contemporary Fenian material contains relatively few references to 1798. See documents in O'Hegarty, *History of Ireland*, pp 411–57; William O'Brien and Desmond Ryan (eds), *Devoy's post bag*, (Dublin, 1948), vol. 1 and 2; and Devoy, *Recollection*, pp 302 and 358. Some examples can be found in their newspaper *The Irish people*, published 1863–5. In an article in 1864 Charles Kickham described the spirit of 'ninety-eight being abroad when the I.R.B. was founded and mentioned Tone's grave at Bodenstown. When Cardinal Cullen denounced the Fenians in 1864 he referred to the bloodshed of 1798 and 1848. O'Hegarty, *History of Ireland*, pp 433, 440.

66 *Speeches from the dock, or protests of Irish freedom* (Dublin, 1867); also Devoy, *Recollections* pp 302, 358.

67 Moody, *Fenian movement*, p. 102. The men of 1848 personally inspired the Fenians, Boyce, *Nationalism*, p. 177.

68 O'Hegarty, *History of Ireland*, p. 414.

69 *Proceedings of the home rule conference held at the Rotunda, Dublin*, 18–21 Nov. 1873, pp 5 and 128.

70 Ibid., p.105; Rev. Patrick Lavelle also referred to armies of redcoats in 1798, p. 145.

71 T.P. O'Connor, *The life of Charles Stewart Parnell* (London, n.d.), pp 12–13; R.B. O'Brien, *The life of Charles Stewart Parnell,1846–1891*, vol. 1 (London, 1899), pp 43–4.

72 T.W. Moody, *Davitt and the Irish revolution, 1846–82* (Oxford, 1981), p. 47.

73 Thomas MacKnight, *Ulster as it is* (London,1896), vol.1, pp 22–3.

74 Ibid., vol. 2, p. 194.

75 Neil Jarman, *Displaying faith: orange, green and trade union banners in Northern Ireland* (Belfast, 1999), pp 34–5.

76 R.R. Madden, *The United Irishmen, their lives and times.* Fourth series, (second edition, London, 1860), pp v–xxvi; R.R. Madden, *Memoirs* (edited by his son, T.M. Madden) (London, 1891), pp 163–5.

77 W.J. Fitzpatrick, *The sham squire; and the informers of 1798* (third edition, Dublin, 1866), p. ix.

78 Reprinted in P.J. Kavanagh, *A popular history of the insurrection of 1798* (third edition, Dublin, 1913), p. vii.

79 *Speeches from the dock*, pp 5–10. Marianne Elliott comments on the significance of this publication in *Tone*, p. 414.

80 See M.J. MacManus, *A bibliography of Wolfe Tone* (Dublin, 1940); R.B. O'Brien, *The autobiography of Theobald Wolfe Tone* (London, 1893).

81 Alice Milligan, *Life of Wolfe Tone* (Belfast, 1898), pp 113–6.

82 Woods, 'Tone's grave', p. 146: *The Weekly Nation*, 26 June 1897.

83 See Jack McCoy, *Ulster's Joan of Arc: an examination of the Betsy Gray story* (Bangor, 1989).

84 Anna Kinsella, '1798 claimed for catholics: Father Kavanagh, Fenians and the centenary celebrations' in Daire Keogh and Nicholas Furlong (eds), *The mighty wave: the 1798 rebellion in Wexford* (Dublin, 1998), p. 146.

85 Gary Owens, 'Nationalist monuments in Ireland, c. 1870–1914: symbolism and ritual' in Raymond Gillespie and Brian Kennedy (eds), *Ireland: art into history* (Dublin, 1994), p. 105.

86 Kinsella, Kavanagh and 1798, p. 146.

87 McCoy, *Betsy Gray*, pp 16–17.

88 T.J. O'Keefe, 'The 1898 efforts to celebrate the United Irishmen: the '98 centennial' in *Eire-Ireland*, vol. xxiii, no. 2 (Summer 1988) pp 53–4.

89 Kinsella, Kavanagh and 1798, pp 149–50

90 See O'Keefe, 'The 1898 efforts', pp 53–4.

91 Senia Paseta, '1798 in 1898: the politics of commemoration' in *Irish Review*, no. 22 (Summer 1998), p. 52.

92 Owens, 'Nationalist monuments', p. 106.

93 O'Keefe, 'The 1898 efforts', p. 55.

94 O'Keefe, 'The 1898 efforts', p. 69.

95 Ibid., pp 67–9.

96 O'Keefe, '"Who fears to speak of '98"', p. 68.

97 Owens, 'Nationalist monuments', pp 107–14.

98 Judith Hill, *Irish public sculpture: a history* (Dublin, 1998), p. 120. See also John Turpin, 'Oliver Sheppard's 1798 memorials' in *Irish Arts Review* (1990–1), pp 71–80.

99 Paseta, '1798 in 1898', p. 49.

100 Owens, 'Nationalist monuments', p. 114; Woods, 'Tone's grave' p.146.

[101] See speeches at Dublin parade to lay the foundation stone for Tone's memorial, *Freeman's Journal*, 16 Aug. 1898.

[102] Turpin, 'Sheppard's memorials', p. 73.

[103] O'Keefe, 'The 1898 efforts', p. 63.

[104] *Belfast Morning News*, 7 June 1898.

[105] Mc Coy, *Betsy Gray*, pp 18–35.

[106] *Belfast News Letter*, 7–11 June 1898.

[107] Ibid., 2 June 1898.

[108] *Belfast News Letter*, 16 Aug. 1898; *Northern Whig*, 16 Aug. 1898, *Irish Times*, 16 Aug. 1898.

[109] *Northern Whig*, 10 June 1898.

[110] Ibid., 9 June 1898.

[111] Milligan, *Tone*, p. 5.

[112] McCoy, *Betsy Gray*, pp 16–35.

[113] Quoted in W.G. Lyttle, *Betsy Gray, or, hearts of Down* (Bangor, 1888; reprint Newcastle, 1968), p. 163.

[114] Collins, 'Contest of memory' p. 43.

[115] Quoted by A.T.Q. Stewart in review in *Irish Times*, 10 Oct. 1998.

[116] F.S.L. Lyons, *Ireland since the Famine* (London, 1971), p. 260.

[117] Helen Litton, *Irish rebellions, 1798–1916, an illustrated history* (Dublin, 1998), p. 94.

[118] The press has few references to Bodenstown from 1898 to 1910.

[119] *United Irishman*, 24 June 1905.

[120] See *Sinn Féin*, 20 June 1908.

[121] Quoted in Nicholas Mansergh, *The Irish Question, 1840–1921* (London, 1965), p. 245.

[122] P.F. Kavanagh, *A popular history of the insurrection of 1798* (third edition, Dublin, 1913); Samuel McSkimin, *Annals of Ulster*, with notes by E.J. McCrum (Belfast, 1906).

[123] F.J. Bigger, *William Orr* (Belfast, 1906).

[124] Cheryl Herr (ed.), *For the land they loved: Irish political melodramas, 1890–1925* (Syracuse, 1992).

[125] Eileen O'Reilly, 'Rebel, muse, and spouse; the female in '98 fiction' in *Eire-Ireland*, vol. xxxiv, no. 2, (Summer 1999), pp 135–54.

[126] Page reproduced in *Causeway* (Spring 1998), p. 50.

[127] Turpin, 'Sheppard's memorials', pp 76–9.

[128] Ibid., p.76.

[129] Ibid., p.78.

[130] L.G. Redmond-Howard in his *John Redmond* (London, 1912), p. 23, quoted Redmond saying, 'For myself, the rising of Wexford County in '98 is one which from my very earliest youth has exercised a powerful fascination upon my mind.'

[131] Owens, 'Nationalist monuments', p. 107.

[132] R.M. Henry, *The evolution of Sinn Féin* (Dublin, 1920), p. 56.

133 John Kelly, 'Parnell in Irish literature' in George Boyce and Alan O'Day (eds), *Parnell in perspective* (London, 1991), p. 265.

134 R.M. Fox, *Green banners* (London,1938), p. 69.

135 Boyce, *Nationalism*, p. 308.

136 A.C. Hepburn, *A past apart; studies in the history of catholic Belfast, 1850–1950* (Belfast, 1996), pp137–72.

137 Jonathan Bardon, *A history of Ulster* (Belfast, 1992), pp 423–4.

138 J.A. Gaughan, (ed.), *Memoirs of Senator Joseph Connolly, a founder of modern Ireland* (Dublin, 1996), p. 75.

139 Ibid., p. 74.

140 J.C. MacDermott, *An enriching life* (Belfast, 1979), p. 25. I am grateful to Professor Paul Bew for drawing my attention to this reference.

141 Gaughan, *Memoirs of Joseph Connolly*, p. 76.

142 Marnie Hay, 'Explaining Uladh: the promotion of nationalism and regionalism in Ulster (M.A. (Irish Studies) thesis, Queen's University of Belfast, 1999).

143 Bulmer Hobson, *Ireland, yesterday and tomorrow* (Tralee, 1968), p. 2.

144 Moody and Martin, *The course of Irish history*, p. 301.

145 R.F. Foster, *Modern Ireland, 1600–1972* (London, 1988), p.432.

146 R. Dudley Edwards, *Patrick Pearse: the triumph of failure* (London,1977), pp 152–93, 250–61, 317–9.

147 Fox, *Green banners*, p. 11.

148 A. Duffin to D. Duffin, 25 Apr.1916, quoted in Patrick Buckland (ed.), *Irish unionism, 1885–1923: a documentary history* (Belfast, 1973) p. 404.

149 Sir Roger Casement to Jack Kelly, n.d., quoted in *Irish Times*,12 Aug. 1999.

150 A.C. Hepburn, *The conflict of nationality in modern Ireland* (London, 1980), p. 111.

151 Richard English, *Ernie O'Malley, IRA intellectual* (Oxford, 1998), p. 112.

152 James Mackey, *Michael Collins – a life* (Scotland, 1996), p. 21.

153 Quoted in P.T. Orr, 'Doing history', p. 215.

154 *Irish Ind.*, 22 June 1925.

155 Ibid., 21 June 1926.

156 Ibid., 23 June 1924.

157 Ibid., 21 June 1926.

158 Ibid., 22 June 1925.

159 Ibid., 23 June 1924.

160 Patrick Murphy, *Oracles of God; the Roman catholic church and Irish politics, 1922–37* (Dublin, 2000) pp 120–1.

161 Bulmer Hobson, *The life of Wolfe Tone* (Dublin, 1920) p. 3.

162 H.M. Hyde, *The rise of Castlereagh* (London, 1933); Rosamund Jacob, *The rise of the United Irishmen, 1791–94* (London, 1937).

163 See Elliott, *Wolfe Tone*, pp 417–8; for catholic clerical criticism of Tone in the 1920s see Murray, *Oracles of God*, p. 23.

164 Leo McCabe, *Wolfe Tone and the United Irishmen. For or against Christ?* (London, 1937); Elliott, *Wolfe Tone*, p. 417.

[165] Denis Ireland, *Patriot adventurer* (London, 1935).

[166] Sean O'Faolain (ed.), *The autobiography of Wolfe Tone* (London, 1937).

[167] Frank MacDermot, *Theobald Wolfe Tone and his times* (London, 1939; Tralee, 1969), introduction and pp. 277–80.

[168] *Irish Ind.*, 23 June 1930.

[169] *Irish Ind.*, 22 June 1931. Lyons, *Ireland since the famine,* p. 503.

[170] *Irish Times*, 20 June 1932.

[171] *Irish Ind.,*19 and 26 June 1933.

[172] *Irish Ind.*, 18 June 1934; *Irish Times*, 25 June 1934.

[173] *Irish Ind.,*17 and 24 June 1934.

[174] *Irish Ind.*, 27 June 1938.

[175] *Irish Times*, 20 June 1932.

[176] *Irish Ind.*, 23 June 1933.

[177] *Irish Ind.*, 23 June 1930.

[178] *Irish Times*, 19 June 1933.

[179] Patrick Byrne, *Memories of the Republican Congress* (n.d.), p. 10.

[180] *Irish Ind.*, 20 June 1938.

[181] See *Irish Ind.* and *Irish Times* over this period.

[182] *Irish Ind.*, 3 Aug. 1948.

[183] *Irish Ind.*, 12 July 1948.

[184] *Irish Ind.*, 23 Aug. 1948.

[185] See *Irish Ind.*, 14 June and 26 July 1948.

[186] *Irish Ind.*, 14 June and 2 Aug. 1948.

[187] *Irish Ind.*, 10 Sept. 1948.

[188] *Irish Ind.*, 18 Sept. 1948.

[189] Cal McCrystal, *Reflections on a quiet rebel* (London, 1997), p. 118.

[190] Interview in *Belfast Telegraph*, 3 April 1997.

[191] Damian Smyth (ed.), *Two plays by John Hewitt* (Belfast, 1999).

[192] *Irish Times,* 22 June 1964.

[193] *Irish Ind.,* 21 June 1956.

[194] *Irish Times,* 20 June 1960.

[195] *Wolfe Tone Annual,* 1948, p.140.

[196] Hill, *Irish public sculpture,* p. 202.

[197] *Irish Times,* 20 Nov. 1967.

[198] *Irish Times, Irish Ind., Irish Press,* 20 Nov. 1967.

[199] Charles Dickson, *The Wexford rising in 1798: its causes and its course* (Tralee, 1955), *Revolt in the north: Antrim and Down in 1798* (Dublin, 1960).

[200] Seosamh O Cuinneagain, *The Tones in a decade of Irish history* (Enniscorthy, 1958).

[201] Mary McNeill, *The life and times of Mary Ann Mc Cracken, 1770–1866.* (Dublin, 1960).

[202] Pakenham, *The year of liberty,* p. 14.

[203] Prionsias Mac Aonghusa and Liam O Riagain (eds) *The best of Tone* (Cork, 1972).

204 See *Irish Times, Irish Ind.* and *Irish Press*, 20 June 1966.

205 See *Irish Press*, 18 and 24 June 1974.

206 Ibid., 23 June 1980.

207 Ibid., 22 June 1981.

208 *Irish Times*, 20 June 1966.

209 Ibid., 24 June, 1968.

210 *Irish Ind.*, 18 June 1973.

211 *Irish Press*, 14 June 1976.

212 *Irish Times*, 23 June 1986, 22 June 1987.

213 *Irish Times*, 20 June 1966; *Irish Ind.* and *Irish Press,* 24 June 1968.

214 *Irish Times*, 19 June 1972.

215 Martin Mansergh (ed.) *The spirit of the nation: the speeches and statements of Charles J. Haughey* (Cork, 1986), pp 672–3.

216 *Irish Ind.*, 18 June 1973.

217 Marilyn Richtarik, 'Living in interesting times: Stewart Parker's *Northern Star*' in J.P. Harrington and E.J. Mitchell (eds), *Politics and performance in contemporary Northern Ireland* (Amherst, 1999), p.7.

218 Tom Dunne, *Theobald Wolfe Tone, colonial outsider* (Cork, 1982); Louis Cullen, 'The 1798 rebellion in its eighteenth century context' in P.J. Corish (ed.), *Radicals, rebels and establishments: historical studies, XV* (Belfast, 1985), pp 91–113.

219 Elliott, *Wolfe Tone*, introduction.

220 Collins, 'Contest of memory', p. 47.

221 A.T.Q. Stewart, *A deeper silence: the hidden origins of the United Irishmen* (London, 1993), *The summer soldiers: the 1798 rebellion in Antrim and Down* (Belfast, 1995).

222 Kevin Whelan, *The year of liberty: radicalism, catholicism and the construction of Irish identity* (Cork, 1996).

223 Ian McBride, 'Reclaiming the rebellion: 1798 in 1998' in *Irish Historical Studies*, vol. xxxi, no. 123, (May, 1999), pp 395–410.

224 Allan Blackstock, *An ascendancy army: the Irish yeomanry, 1796–1834*(Dublin, 1998).

225 See Keogh and Furlong, *The mighty wave;* Tom Dunne, 'Wexford's Comoradh '98: politics, heritage and history' in *History Ireland*, vol. 6, no. 2 (Summer, 1998), pp 49–53. See also Tom Dunne, 'Dangers lie in the romanticizing of 1798' in *Irish Times*, 6 Jan. 1998.

226 Tom Bartlett, (ed.), *Life of Theobald Wolfe Tone*, compiled and arranged by William Theobald Wolfe Tone (Dublin, 1998).

227 Christopher Woods, R.B. McDowell and T.W. Moody (eds), *The writings of T.W. Tone, 1763–98*, vol 1 (Oxford, 1998).

228 W.A. Maguire (ed.), *Up in arms: the 1798 bicentenary rebellion in Ireland, a bicentenary exhibition* (Belfast, 1998).

229 'An Irishwoman's diary', by Yvonne Healy, *Irish Times*, 21 July 1995.

230 Collins, 'Contest of memory', pp 49–50.

231 *Irish Times*, 9 Sept. 1998.

232 *Irish Ind.*, 23 May 1998.

233 Forde, *From heritage to hope*, p. 6.

234 *Irish Times*, 19 Oct. 1998.

235 Ibid., 22 June 1998; *An Phoblacht*, 23 April 1998.

236 Collins, 'Contest of memory', pp 48–9.

237 *Irish Times*, 4 Dec. 1998.

238 Collins, 'Contest of memory', p. 50.

CHAPTER 3

1 *Northern Ireland Parliament*, vol. II, 15 July 1922; vol. VI, 19 May 1925.

2 Public Record Office of Northern Ireland, CAB/4/125, no. 8, 20 Oct. 1924; CAB/4/147, no. 2, 10 Aug. 1925.

3 *Northern Whig*, 13 July, 1922.

4 Ibid., 13 July 1923.

5 Ibid., 14 July 1925.

6 Ibid., 13 July 1926.

7 Ibid., 13 July 1927.

8 A.D. McDonnell, *The life of Sir Denis Henry, catholic unionist* (Belfast, 2000).

9 Jonathan Bardon, *A history of Ulster* (Belfast, 1992), p. 511.

10 Keith Jeffery, 'Parades, police and government in Northern Ireland, 1922–69' in T.G. Fraser (ed.), *The Irish parading tradition: following the drum* (London, 2000), pp 84–6.

11 *Northern Whig*, 13 July 1933.

12 Ibid., 13 July 1932.

13 Ibid., 13 July 1939.

14 *Portadown News*, 13 July 1940, 12 July 1941, 4, 18 July 1942, 17 July 1943.

15 *Northern Whig*, 13 July 1955, 14 July 1958.

16 Ibid., 12 July 1960.

17 Ibid., 13 July 1960 and 13 July 1961.

18 Ibid, 13 July 1960.

19 *Irish Times*, 12 Nov. 1919.

20 Jane Leonard, *The culture of commemoration: the culture of war commemoration* (Dublin, 1996), p. 20.

21 *Irish News*, 12 Nov. 1924.

22 Keith Jeffery, 'The Great War in modern Irish memory' in T.G. Fraser and Keith Jeffery (eds), *Men, women and war: historical studies*, xviii (Dublin, 1993), p. 151.

23 Leonard, *Culture of commemoration*, p. 20.

24 Keith Jeffery, *Ireland and the Great War* (Cambridge, 2000), p. 133.

25 Jeffery, *The Great War in memory*, p. 150.

26 Ibid., pp 150–1.

27 *Belfast Telegraph*, 11 Nov. 1930.

28 *Belfast News Letter*, 11 Nov. 1937; *Londonderry Sentinel*, 13 Nov. 1934.

29 *Belfast News Letter*, 11 Nov. 1946, 13 Nov. 1950.

30 Ibid., 11, 12 Nov. 1955; 11, 12 Nov. 1956; *Northern Whig*, 11, 12 Nov. 1955, 11, 12 Nov. 1956; *Irish News,* 11, 12 Nov. 1955, 11, 12 Nov. 1956.

31 *Northern Whig*, 18 March 1930.

32 Rex Cathcart, *The most contrary region: the BBC in Northern Ireland, 1924–84* (Belfast, 1984), p. 32.

33 *Irish News*, 18 March 1932; *Belfast News Letter*, 17 March 1932.

34 *Northern Whig*, 18 March 1930.

35 *Belfast News Letter*, 18 March 1946, 18 March 1950, 17 March 1952.

36 Document is quoted in *Belfast News Letter*, 1 January 1996.

37 *Irish Ind.*, 18 March 1954; for complaints about schools not closing see *Belfast News Letter*, 16 March 1961.

38 Ibid., 17 March 1961.

39 *Belfast Telegraph*, 17 March 1956.

40 *Belfast News Letter*, 17 March 1961.

41 *Irish Ind.*, 19 March 1956; *Belfast Telegraph*, 10 March 1964.

42 *Northern Ireland Parliament*, vol. ix, 15 May 1928.

43 Ibid., vol. xiv, 22 March 1932.

44 See Neil Jarman and Dominic Bryan, 'Green parades in an Orange state' in Fraser, *The Irish parading tradition*, pp 95–110.

45 *Irish News*, 22 April 1935.

46 Ibid., 17 April 1933.

47 Ibid., 6 April 1942.

48 Ibid., 10 April 1950.

49 Jarman and Bryan, 'Green parades', pp 103–5.

50 *Irish Ind.*, 18 March 1926.

51 Ibid., 16 March 1930.

52 Ibid., 18 March 1931.

53 Ibid., 18 March 1932, 19 March 1934.

54 See speech by Eamon de Valera in Maurice Moynihan (ed.), *Speeches and statements by Eamon de Valera* (Dublin, 1980), pp 217–9.

55 *Irish Ind.*, 18 March 1935.

56 *Northern Whig*, 18 March 1939.

57 *Irish Ind.*, 18 March 1939.

58 Moynihan, *De Valera's speeches*, p. 46.

59 *Irish Ind.*, 18 March 1950.

60 Ibid., 18 March 1953.

61 Ibid., 18 March 1955.

62 *Capuchin Annual*, (1961), p. 218.

63 See Rosemary Ryan (et al.), 'Commemorating 1916' in *Retrospect* (1984), pp 59–62.

[64] David Fitzpatrick, 'Commemorating in the Irish Free State: a chronicle of embarrassment' in Ian McBride (ed.), *Commemorations in Ireland* (Cambridge, forthcoming).

[65] *Irish Ind.*, 2 April 1934.

[66] Fitzpatrick, 'Commemorating in the Irish Free State'.

[67] *Irish Ind.*, 5 April 1935.

[68] Judith Hill, *Irish public sculpture* (Dublin, 1998), pp 188–9.

[69] *Irish Ind.*, 14 April 1941.

[70] Ibid., 19 April 1954.

[71] Ryan, 'Commemorating 1916', p. 61.

[72] Jane Leonard, 'The twinge of memory: armistice day and remembrance Sunday in Dublin since 1919' in Richard English and Graham Walker (eds), *Unionism in modern Ireland* (Dublin, 1996), p. 101.

[73] Ibid.

[74] Hill, *Irish sculpture*, pp 189–90.

[75] See Jeffery, *Ireland and the Great War*, pp 107–23.

[76] *Irish News*, 12 Nov. 1924.

[77] Leonard, *Armistice Day in Dublin*, 105.

[78] Brian Hanley, 'Poppy day in Dublin in the '20s and '30s in *History Ireland*, vol. 7, no. 1. (Spring 1999), pp 5–6.

[79] Leonard, 'Armistice Day in Dublin', p. 106.

[80] Fitzpatrick, 'Commemorating in the Irish Free State'.

[81] Ibid.

[82] Brian Girvin and Geoffrey Roberts, 'The forgotten volunteers of World War II' in *History Ireland*, vol. 6, no. 1 (Spring 1998), pp 46–51.

[83] *Belfast News Letter*, 13 Nov. 1950.

[84] Jane Leonard, 'Facing the "finger of scorn": Veterans' memories of Ireland after the Great War' in Martin Evans and Kenneth Lunn (eds), *War and memory in the twentieth century* (Oxford, 1997), pp 59–72.

[85] *Northern Whig*, 13 July 1923.

[86] Ibid., 14 July 1925.

[87] Ibid., 14 July 1930.

[88] *Londonderry Sentinel*, 15 July 1930.

[89] *Northern Whig*, 14 July 1931.

[90] Ibid.; *Irish Ind.*, 13 Aug. 1931.

[91] Aiken McClelland, 'Orangeism in Co. Monaghan' in *Clogher Record* (1978), pp 401–2.

[92] Special meeting of the County Monaghan Grand Orange Lodge, 28 June 1932, recorded in minutes of the County Monaghan Grand Orange Lodge, May 1932–May 1943 (in private possession).

[93] Recorded in above minutes.

[94] *Belfast News Letter*, 11 July 1936.

[95] Jeffery, *Ireland and the Great War*, p.107, This comment about 11 Nov. was made by General Sir William Hickie.

96 See Craig's comments in 1934 and 1938. Dennis Kennedy, *The widening gulf: northern attitudes to the independent Irish state, 1919–49* (Belfast, 1988), pp 166 and 173–4.

97 Paul Arthur, *Political realities, government and politics of Northern Ireland* (London, 1980), p.92. Kenneth Bloomfield, *Stormont in crisis: a memoir* (Belfast, 1994).

CHAPTER 4

1 *Report of the international body on decommissioning*, 22 January 1996 (Belfast and Dublin, 1996), p. 5.

2 *Report of the independent review of parades and marches*, 1997 (Belfast, 1997), p. 29.

3 See *Irish Times*, 18 May 1998.

4 *Belfast Telegraph*, 8 April 1998.

5 *Irish Times*, 5 Sept. 1998.

6 Liam Kennedy, *Colonialism, religion and nationalism in Ireland* (Belfast, 1996), p. 221.

7 See S.M. Lipset and Stein Rokkan, 'Cleavage structures, party systems and voter alignment: an introduction' in Lipset and Rokkan (eds), *Party systems and voter alignment* (New York, 1967), pp50–6; Gordon Smith, *Politics in Western Europe* (London, 1972; 4th edition, London, 1983), pp 12–14, 44–6; A.R. Ball, *Modern politics and government* (London, 1988), pp 82–4.

8 See Martin Mansergh, 'the 1798 rebellion and its meaning for today' in Walter Forde (ed.), *From heritage to hope* (Gorey, Co.Wexford, 1998), p. 37. David Trimble, *The foundation of Northern Ireland* (Lurgan, 1991), p.1.

9 *Irish Times*, 18 Mar. 1999.

10 David Fitzpatrick, 'A failed experiment in Irish education' in Ciaran Brady (ed.), *Ideology and the historians*, (Dublin, 1991), pp 174–83.

11 Ibid., p. 181.

12 Jack Magee, 'Are there any remedies?' in W.J.N. Mackey (The Churches Central Committee for Community Work), *Irish history: fact or fiction* (Belfast, 1976) pp 13.

13 *Irish Times*, 25 Feb. 1998.

14 Robert Greacen, *The sash my father wore; an autobiography* (Edinburgh, 1997), p. 34.

15 Quoted in Dominic Bryan, *Orange parades: the politics of ritual, tradition and control* (London, 2000), pp 162–3.

16 See B.M. Walker, *Dancing to history's tune* (Belfast, 1996), pp 1–33.

17 *Hansard*, lxxxvii, (1985–6), 779, 783, 904 and 907.

18 Alvin Jackson, 'Unionist myths 1912–85' in *Past and Present* no.136 (August, 1992), pp 164–85.

19 See Steve Bruce, *The red hand: protestant paramilitaries in Northern Ireland* (Oxford, 1992), pp 233–5.

[20] Article by Cromyln in *Church of Ireland Gazette*, 13 January 1995.

[21] *Irish Times*, 13 April 1994.

[22] Interview in *Irish Times*, 3 March 1994.

[23] Neil Jarman, *Displaying faith: Orange, green and trade union banners in Northern Ireland* (Belfast, 1999), pp 33–6.

[24] *Irish Ind.*, 15 June 1953.

[25] See articles and letters in *Belfast Telegraph*, 3 and 11 June 1996.

[26] See *Hansard*, lxxxvii, (1985–6) 779, 783, 904 and 907.

[27] Shane O'Doherty, *The volunteer: a former I.R.A. man's true story* (London, 1993), pp 27–30.

[28] *Irish Times*, 18 Dec. 1993.

[29] *Report of the international body on decommissioning*, p 5.

[30] See Gordon Smyth, *Politics in Western Europe* (London, 1972; fifth edition, 1990), pp19–28, 353–85, 367–70. Alf Kaartvedt, 'The economic basis of Norwegian nationalism in the nineteenth century' in Rosalind Mitchison (ed.) *The roots of nationalism: studies in northern Europe* (Edinburgh, 1980), pp11–19.

[31] J. Bowyer Bell, *The Irish troubles: a generation of violence, 1967–92* (Dublin, 1993), p. 829.

[32] A local PACE group organised a conference at Portadown in November 1991 to look at the 1641 massacres. See Brigid Lenane, *The state we're in: How can we change it?* (The churches' peace education programme, Belfast 1996). Another example has been the annual series of Irish history lectures, known as the Rockwell lectures, run for schoolchildren at Queen's University, Belfast, by Bishop Gordon McMullan between 1990 and 2000.

[33] Jonathan Bardon, *A history of Ulster* (Belfast, 1992).

[34] Marianne Elliott, *Wolfe Tone: prophet of Irish independence* (New Haven, 1989); Tim Pat Coogan, *De Valera: Long fellow, long shadow* (London, 1993); Alvin Jackson, *Sir Edward Carson* (Dundalk, 1993).

[35] Jane Leonard, *The culture of commemoration: the culture of war commemoration* (Dublin, 1997), p21–2.

[36] Brian Girvin and Geoffrey Roberts, 'The forgotten volunteers of World War II' in *History Ireland*, vol. 6, no. 1 (Spring, 1998), pp 46–51.

[37] *Irish Times*, 14 Sept. 1998.

[38] *Irish Times*, 14 November, 1998.

[39] *Belfast Telegraph*, 2 July 1992.

[40] *Anglo-Irish Agreement, 1985* (Dublin, 1985).

[41] *Joint Declaration, Downing Street, 1993.*

[42] *Frameworks for the future,*1995.

[43] Sir Patrick Mayhew, 'Culture and identity', 16 December (1992) (Northern Ireland Information Service).

[44] *Irish Times*, 6 Feb. 1993.

[45] *Irish Independent*, 14 Nov. 1992.

[46] *Irish Times*, 19 April 1993.

[47] Ibid., 8 Nov. 1993.

[48] *Irish Ind.*, 5 April, 19 June 1993.

[49] *Irish News*, 31 Dec. 1992.

[50] *Sunday Times*, 7 Mar. 1993.

[51] *Irish News*, 16 Feb. 1993.

[52] *Irish Times*, 23 March, 19 April 1993.

[53] Ibid., 8 April 1993.

[54] Ibid., 2 October 1993.

[55] George Drower, *John Hume: peacemaker* (London, 1995), pp. 167–8.

[56] *Observer*, 4 Sept. 1994

[57] *Irish Times*, 26 May 1994.

[58] *Irish News*, 6 Jan. 1994.

[59] Ibid., 1 Sept. 1994.

[60] Ibid.

[61] *Combat*, Oct. 1994.

[62] *Belfast Telegraph*, 19 Sept. 1995; *Irish Ind.*, 30 July 1996.

[63] *Irish Times*, 22 Dec. 1995.

[64] Ibid., 2 Dec. 1995, 4 Mar. 1996.

[65] *Report of the international body on decommissioning*, 22 Jan. 1996 (Dublin and Belfast, 1996), p. 5.

[66] Report of the independent review of parades and marches, Jan. 1997 (Belfast, 1997).

[67] *Sunday Times*, 5 Mar. 1995; *Belfast Telegraph*, 9 June 1995.

[68] *Irish Times*, 14 Aug. 1996.

[69] *Belfast News Letter*, 10 Feb. 1995.

[70] Speech by Ian Paisley at party conference, 25 Nov. 1995 (Linen Hall Library Political Collection)

[71] C.A.M. Noble and I.R.K. Paisley, *Understanding Northern Ireland: an introduction for Americans* (Belfast, 1995).

[72] *Irish Times*, 28 Dec. 1995.

[73] *Irish News*, 4 Feb. 1998.

[74] *Irish Times*, 27 Feb. 1995. Speech by Gerry Adams 1996 ard fheis; speech by Pat Doherty, 1997 ard fheis (Northern Ireland Political Collection, Linen Hall Library).

[75] *Belfast Telegraph*, 27 Dec. 1995.

[76] *Irish Times*, 11 April 1998.

[77] *Belfast Telegraph*, 21 May 1998.

[78] *Ibid.*, 8 April 1998.

[79] *Times*, 5 Sept. 1998.

[80] Human Rights Watch, *Leave none to tell the story: genocide in Rwanda*, (New York, 1999), p. 31.

[81] Fintan O'Toole, *Irish Times*, 30 April 1999. See also Branimir Anzulovic, *Heavenly Serbia: from myth to genocide*, (London, 1999), and Noel Malcolm, *Bosnia: a short history* (London, 1994; 1996 corrected version).

INDEX

Abercorn, Duke of, 87
Act of Union, 41
Adams, Gerry, 74, 115, 116, 118
Adamson, Ian, 108
Aegean, 119
Africa, 119
Ahern, Bertie, 74, 76, 96, 119
Allen, W., 46
All Ireland '98 Commemoration
   Association, 63
America, 40
Ancient Order of Hibernians, 55, 84, 86,
   87, 109
Andrews, James, 65, 65
Andrews, J.A., 65
Anglo-Irish agreement, (1985), 107, 112
Anglo-Irish treaty, (1921), 92
Anglo-Normans, 69, 119
Antrim
   battle of, 48
Apprentice Boys of Derry, 106
   Belfast and District Amalagamated
     Committee, 14
   clubs, 12, 13–15, 19–21, 109
     Baker Club, 14
     Browning Club, 7, 15, 19
     Campsie Club, 19
     Club, 6, 7
     Murray Club
     No Surrender Club, 6, 7
     Walker Club, 7
     Scottish clubs, 21, 22
   Memorial Hall, 8

Mid-Ulster Amalgamated Committee,
   15
   Scottish amalgamated committee, 19
Arbour Hill, Dublin. 93
Armistice Day, 84, 85, 86, 94, 95, 96,.
   99, 100
Australia, 73, 91
   Sydney, 29, 73

B.B.C., 87, 101
Ballinamuck, County Longford, battle
   of, 60
Ballymena Observer, 44
Ballynahinch, County Down, 74,
   battle of, 42, 44, 49, 74
Bardon, Jonathan, 2
Barry, Kevin, 58
Bartlett, Tom, 72
Bastille Day, 79
Bates, Sir Dawson, 15
Bates R.D., 81
Belfast
   Agreement, 74, 116, 118–20
   City Council, 73, 74, 111
   City Hall, 85
Belfast Magazine, 36
Belfast News Letter, 10, 49, 83, 86, 87
Belfast Telegraph, 88, 102, 107, 119
Bell, J. Bowyer, 111
Bell, Sam Hanna, 71
Benn, George, 36
Bigger, Francis Joseph, 53, 56
Birch, Rev.T.L., 35

Black see Royal Black Institution
Blackstock, Allan, 72
Blair, Tony, 119
Bodenstown, County Kildare, 38, 43, 44, 48, 57, 58–61, 66, 69, 70, 74, 75
Boer War, 52
Boolavogue, County Wexford, 45
'Boolavogue', 31
Bourke, P.J., 53
Boyne, battle 0f, 2, 80, 99, 106, 107, 108, 114, 118
British
    army, 62
    empire, 83
British Legion, 95
Brookeborough, Lord, (Basil Brooke, Viscount), 20, 83, 87
Brugha, Ruairí Brugha, 70
Burnside, Sam, 3
Byrne, Myles, 67

Canterbury, Archbishop of, 88
Cameron Ferguson, publishers, 53
Canada, 1, 13, 81
Capuchin Annual, 92
Carson, Edward, 108
Casement, Sir Roger, 30, 56, 57, 109
Cassidy, Michael, 101
Castlereagh, Lord, (Robert Stewart, Viscount), 60
Cathleen ni Houlihan, 53, 109
Caitlín Ni Houlihan, 109
Caulfield, James, 35
Chart, D.A., 105
Christmas Day, 79
Clann na Poblachta, 66
Clarke, Kathleen, 67
Clarke, Tom, 67
Clinch, James, 3
Clinton, President William, 102–3, 116–17, 119, 120
Cobain, Fred, 73
Collins, Michael, 58, 59, 84
Communism
    Irish communist party, 61
Community Relations Council, 73, 74, 111
Comoradh '98, 73
Connaught Rangers, 85
Connolly, James, 57, 115
Connolly, Joseph, 56

Conway, Michael, 63
Coogan, Tim Pat, 111
Cooke, Henry, 33
Corrigan, S.L., 37
Cosgrave, William Thomas, 58, 59, 90–1, 95
Costello, John, 64
Costello, J.A., 92, 94
Costello, Seamus, 70
Covenant Day, 56
Craig, Sir James, 80–3, 85, 107
Cullen, Louis, 71
Cullen, Luke, 32
Cumann na Gaedheal, 62, 93
Cumann na mBan, 59

Davis, Thomas, 32, 38, 40, 54, 57
Davitt, Michael, 41
Decommissioning see International body on decommissioning
Defenderism, 32
Denny, Fr Aidan, 115
Derry, siege of, 108, 114, 118
Delaney, Edward, 67
Democratic Unionist Party, (D.U.P.), 101, 118
de Valera, Eamon, 59, 61, 64, 67, 68, 91, 92, 93, 95
Devlin, Anne, 32
Devlin, Bernadette, 108
Devlin, Joseph, 48, 55
Devoy, John, 31, 40
Diamond, Harry, 90
Dickson, Charles, 68
Dickson, Rev. Steele, 36, 56
Dillon, John, 46, 48, 49
Dixon, R.S., 83
Down Recorder, 37
Downing Street Joint Declaration, (1993), 112, 113, 115, 116
Drennan, William, 57, 65
Drumcree see Orange Order
Dublin Rising, 1916 see Easter Rising 1916
Duffin, Adam, 57
Duffy, Charles Gavan, 34
Duffy, Fr John, 112
Dungannon Clubs, 56
Dunlop, John, 114
Dunne, Tom, 71, 72

Easter Monday, 79, 80
Easter Rising, (1916), 57, 58, 80, 85, 99, 108, 110, 116
commemorations, 89, 90, 92–4
Edgar, Rev. Samuel, 36
Elliott, Marianne, 71
author, *Wolfe Tone*, 111
Emmet, Robert, 30, 32, 42, 52, 54, 55, 57, 58
Ervine, David, 117
Eucharistic Congress, 91

Famine, Great, 77
Faulkner, Brian, 20
Fernhill House, Belfast, 116
Fenians, 43, 48, 54
Fenianism, 44
Ferguson, J.C., 9
Fianna Fáil, 59, 61, 66, 69, 70, 91, 93, 94, 95, 114
First world war, 94, 112
Fitzgerald, Lord Edward, 52, 58
Fitzpatrick, W.J., 42, 43,
Foresters see Irish National Foresters
Frameworks for the future, (1995), 112, 113, 116
France, 73
Fraser, Tom, 2
Freeman's Journal, 47

Gaelic Association, County Kildare, 52
Gaelic Athletic Association (G.A.A.)
Clubs, 109
Gaelic League, 90, 109
Garland, Sean, 70
Garvaghy Road, Portadown, County Armagh, 74
General Post Office, Dublin, 93
Germany, 103
Gladstone, William Ewart, 42
Glanevin cemetry, Dublin, 93
Grattan, Henry, 54
Greacen, Robert, 106
Grey, Betsy, 45
Grey, Charles, 41
Griffith, Arthur, 54, 56

Hamilton Rowan, 58
Harte, Chris, 115
Hartley, Tom, 112, 116
Haughey, Charles, 71

Hay, Edward, 35
Henry, Sir Denis, 82
Henry, Dr Henry, 55
Hewitt, John, 66
Hibernians see Ancient Order of Hibernians
Hobsbawm, Eric, 26, 27
Hobson, Bulmer, 56, 57, 60
Holland, 104, 110
Hope, (James), Jemmy, 30, 56, 65, 71
Hume, John, 101, 108, 109, 115, 118
Hungary, 103
Hyde, Douglas, 91, 94

Independence Day, 79
Indian, sub-continent, 119
Ingram, John Kells, 37
International body on decommissioning, 101
Ireland, Denis, 61
Iris, 110
16th (Irish) Division, 85
Irish Freedom, 57
Irish Independent, 58, 61, 68
Irish National Foresters, 42, 109
Irish National War Memorial Park, Islandbridge, Dublin, 111
See also Islandbridge
Irish News, 55, 84–5, 86, 109, 116
Irish Parliamentary Party
Anti-Parnellite wing, 46
Irish Press, 68
Irish Republican Army, (I.R.A.), 61, 62, 63, 75, 83, 89, 97, 110, 115, 116, 117, 118–9
old IRA, 90, 93
Irish Republican Brotherhood, (I.R.B.), 31, 40, 43, 46, 48, 55, 56
Irish Times, 49, 63, 68, 84, 102, 119
Irish Weekly, 53
Islandbridge, Dublin, 95, 96, see also Irish National War Memorial Park
Italy, 104, 110

Jackson, Alvin, author, *Sir Edward Carson*, 111
Jeffery, Keith, 85
Johnston, J.M., 36
Johnston, William, 8, 9

Kane, Rev. James, 22

Kavanagh, Fr Patrick, 43, 48, 53, 54
Keenan, Sean, 70
Kennedy, Liam, 103
Kennedy, M.J., 60
Keery, Neville, 71
Keville, Fr John, 60
King James I, 106
King William III, 106
Kosovo, 121

Linen Hall Library, Belfast, 74
Londonderry Journal, 4
Londonderry, Lord, (Charles Stewart
    Henry, 7th marquis), 82
Londonderry Sentinel, 9, 15, 16, 18, 19,
    24
Londonderry Standard, 5
Londonderry Temperance Council, 18
Longford, Lord, 60
Lucy, Cornelius, 92
Lynch, Jack, 68

Lacey, Patrick, 67
Lacey, Philip, 67
Lalor, James Fintan, 38, 57
Latimer, W.T., 44
Lemass, Sean, 67
Leonard, Jane, 94
Loudan, Jack, 66
Lisnaskea, 11
Little, Dr James, 16
Liverpool, 53
Lough Swilly Company, 20
Lundy, Col. Robert, 2, 4, 10
Lyttle, W.G., 44, 45

MacAonghusa, Prionsias, 69
MacDermot, Frank, 61
MacDermott, J.C., 56
MacDermott, Sean, 55
MacEntee, Sean, 92
MacKnight, Thomas, 41, 42
MacManaway, J.G., 18
MacSwiney, Terence, 65
McAleese, President, Mary, 29, 73, 112
McArt's Fort, 46, 55
McBride, Ian, 3
McBride, Sean, 61, 64
McCabe, Leo, 61
McClelland, Aiken, 7
McConnell, Joseph, 53

McCracken, Henry Joy, 42, 56, 65, 69,
    71, 106
McCracken, Mary Ann, 33, 36, 69
McCrystal, Cal, 65
McCrystal, Cathal, 65
McCusker, Harold, 107
McDowell, R.B., 72
McGuiness, 118
McKittrick, David, 2
McLaughlin, 118
McMichael, Gary, 117
McNeill, Mary, 69
McSkimin, Samuel, 37, 44
Madden, J.A., 59
Madden, R.R., 35, 42, 43, 44
Magee, Jack, 106
Magennis, James, (V.C.), 111
Maginnis, Ken, 114
Maguire, W.A., 72
Mayhew, Sir Patrick, 113, 116
Major, John, 113, 116
Malan, Rian, 115
Mallon, Seamus, 115
Manchester Martyrs, 40, 68
Markievicz, Countess Constance, 59
Maxwell, W.H., 34
May Day, 79
May, W.M., 84
Melbourne, Lord, 41
Michelburne, Col., 3
Middle East, 119
Milligan, Alice, 44
Milligan, C.D., 3
Mitchel, John, 38,41, 54
Mitchell commission, (1996), 110
Mitchell, Gary, 106
Mitchell, George, 117
Monmartre Cemetry, Paris, 67
Monro, Henry, 32
Montgomery, Henry, 33
Moody, T.W., 72
Moore, Maurice, 95
Mountjoy, 5, 8, 22
Murphy, Fr Patrick, 64
Murray, Dennis, 101
Musgrave, Sir Richard, 34, 35

Na Fianna Éireann, 55, 56
    clubs
        Betsy Grays, 55
        McCrackens, 55

Neilsons, 55
O'Neills, 55
Orrs, 55
Tones, 55
Nation, The, 37
National Commemoration Committee, 93
National Graves Association, 59, 89
Neilson, Samuel, 35, 56
Nelson, Rev. Isaac, 41
Newtownbarry, County Wexford, St Mary's cemetery, 45
Newtownbutler, County Fermanagh, 11, 17, battle of, 11, 23
New Ulster Defender, 108
North, Peter, 117
Northern Star, 55
Northern Whig, 9, 10, 13, 41, 49, 83, 86
Norton, William, 64
No Surrender Club see Apprentice Boys of Derry
Nicholson, William, 3
Norway, 104, 110
Nugent, Major General Sir Oliver, 84

O'Brien, R. Barry, 41
O'Brien, William Smith, 39
O'Connell, Daniel, 32, 37, 40, 42, 54, 118
O'Connellite movement, 37
O'Connor, T.P., 41
O Cuinneagain, Seosamh, 69
O'Donnell, Cardinal Patrick, 85
O'Donoghue, M.V., 109
O'Faolain, Sean, 61
Official Sinn Féin see Sinn Féin
O'Higgins, Brian, 59, 60
O'Keefe, Timothy, 46
O'Kelly, President Sean T., 64, 94
O'Leary, John, 48, 52
O'Malley, Ernie, 58
O'Neill, Hugh, 91
O'Neill, Owen Roe, 38
O'Neill, Captain Terence, 20
Omagh, Co. Tyrone, bomb, 29, 119
Orange Order, 16, 37, 75, 80–3, 84, 98, 106, 109
demonstrations, 84
dinner, 10
Drumcree, County Armagh, 83
hall, Portadown, 10

Junior, Association, 17
lodges, 15
marches and parades, 10, 96, 97, 98
Garvaghy Road, 74
Orangeism, 42
Orangemen, 17, 23
parades, 14
protesters, 49
Scottish branches, 14
speeches, 82
See also Twelfth of July
Ordnance Survey memoirs, 6
O Riagain, Liam, 69
Orr, William, 32, 42, 56, 74

Paisley, Ian, 101, 115, 118, 119
Pakenham, Thomas, 69
Palmerston, Lord, 41
Parker, Stewart, 71
Parnell, Charles Stewart, 41, 47, 52, 54, 109
Parnellite split, 45
Party Processions Act, 7
Paxman, Jeremy, 101
Pearse, Patrick, 57, 75, 105, 115, 116
Pender, M.T., 53
Phoblacht, An, 110
Phoenix Park, Dublin, 96
Pope Pius IX, 42
Price, W.H., 15
Progressive Unionist Party, (P.U.P.), 117
Protestant and Catholic Encounter, 111
Provisional Sinn Féin see Sinn Féin

Queen's Royal Theatre, Dublin, 53
Queen Victoria, 39, 46, 87

Radio Éireann, 93
Rebellion, 1641, 2
massacres, 118
Redmond, John, 47, 51, 53, 54
Redmond, William, 54
Remembrance
Day, 79, 86, 111, 121
Sunday, 96
Republican Congress, 61, 62, 63
Republic of Ireland Act, 66
Reynolds, Albert, 113, 114
Ribbonmen, 31
Ribbonism, 33
Robinson, Peter, 23, 107

Rome, 92
Rowan, Archibald Hamilton, 36
Royal Black Institution, 15, 16, 17, 23, 97, 98
Royal Ulster Constabulary, 90
Russell, Lord John, 41
Russell, Sean, 62
Russell, Thomas, 34
Rwanda, 120

Saintfield, County Down, battle of, 32
Saint Patrick's Day, 80, 86–8, 90–2, 99, 100, 117
Sampson, Rev. George Vaughan, 5
Sands, Bobby, 115
Scotland, 13, 22
Second world war, 77, 112
Shaw, George Bernard, 51
Sheppard, Oliver, 53
Simms, George Otto, 68
Sinn Féin, 54, 55, 57, 59, 71, 75, 93, 110, 112, 115, 118
  (Gardner Place), 69
  (Kevin Street), 69
  Official, 70
  Provisional, 69, 70
Smith, Rev. W.J., 44
Social Democratic and Labour Party, (S.D.L.P.), 101, 115, 118
Somme, Battle, 85, 108
Special Powers Act, 89
Spence, Gusty, 65
Spender, Wilfred, 107
Spring, Dick, 114
Stewart, A.T.Q., 2, 72
Sunday Times, 114
Switzerland, 104, 110
Sydney, Australia, 29

Tandy, Napper, 58
Teeling, Charles Hamilton, 34, 36
Templepatrick, County Antrim, parish of, 33
Test Act, 1704, 4
Thompson, James, 36
Tone, Wolfe, 30, 34, 35, 37, 38, 41, 43, 46, 47, 49, 52, 55–61, 63, 65, 68, 70, 72, 74, 75, 105, 106
  clubs, 68
  See also Bodenstown
Tóstal, An, 94

Trimble, David, 104
Trimble, W.C., 17
Twelfth of July, 80–3, 97, 100, 106
Twomey, Maurice, 63

Uladh, 56
Ulster Monthly Magazine, 36
Ulster Museum, 74
36th (Ulster) Division, 84
Ulster Unionist
  Council, 13, 20, 21
  leader, 104
  Party, 118
Ulster Transport Authority, 20
Ulster Volunteer Force, (U.V.F.), 65, 116
Union, Act of, 41
United Irish Commemorative Society, 73, 74
United Irish League, 55
United Irishman, 38, 54
United States of America, 73, 81, 91

Victoria, Queen see Queen Victoria
Vinegar Hill, County Wexford, battle of, 31, 45, 62

Walker, Cecil, 118
Walker, Rev. George, 5
  monument, 21
Warnock, Edmond, 64, 65
Washington, U.S.A., 104
Westminster, 54
Wexford County Council, 73
Whelan, Kevin, 72
Whitbread, J.W., 53
Wilton, J.M., 15
Wolfe Tone Annual, 60
Woods, Christopher, 72

Yeats, W.B., 46, 52
York Fencible Infantry, 32
Young Ireland, 37, 38, 43, 109
  League, 45
  memorial, 44
Young, R.M., 44
Young Unionists' Conference, 88
Yugoslavia, former, 120